SELECTED POEMS OF
EMILY DICKINSON

THE POETRY BOOKSHELF

General Editor: James Reeves

SELECTED POEMS OF

EMILY DICKINSON

Edited with an Introduction
and Notes
by

JAMES REEVES

HEINEMANN

Heinemann Educational Books Ltd
Halley Court, Jordan Hill, Oxford OX2 8EJ

OXFORD LONDON EDINBURGH MELBOURNE SYDNEY
AUCKLAND IBADAN NAIROBI GABORONE HARARE
KINGSTON PORTSMOUTH NH (USA) SINGAPORE MADRID

ISBN 0 435 15023 5 (paperback)

EMILY DICKINSON 1830–1886
INTRODUCTION AND NOTES © JAMES REEVES 1959
FIRST PUBLISHED 1959
REPRINTED 1960, 1963, 1966, 1970, 1973, 1976, 1988, 1989, 1991

Printed in Hong Kong by Dah Hua Printing Press Co. Ltd.

CONTENTS

CONTENTS

PREFACE

THE present selection of Emily Dickinson's poems, about one-tenth of the total, has been made possible by the appearance in 1955 of the Belknap Press edition in three volumes, edited by Thomas H. Johnson and published by the Harvard University Press. For permission to use the text of this edition, including three copyright poems (Nos. 49, 69 and 173 in the present selection) and to adopt Mr. Johnson's chronology I am indebted to Harvard University Press. I have to thank Messrs. Little, Brown & Co., Boston, for permission to include two other copyright poems, Nos. 92 and 110, and Messrs. Houghton Mifflin Co., Boston, for permission to include No. 136.

The portrait of Emily Dickinson at about seventeen years old, which is reproduced as a frontispiece, is included by kind permission of the Houghton Library, Harvard University. No portrait is known to exist showing the poet at a later age.

No editor of Emily Dickinson can fail to be indebted to Mr. Johnson for his immaculate definitive edition of the poems. I am grateful also for his *Emily Dickinson: An Interpretive Biography* (Harvard, 1955). For the facts of Emily Dickinson's life and times I have drawn upon this, as also upon *This Was a Poet* by George F. Whicher (Scribners, 1938) and *Emily Dickinson Face to Face* by Martha Dickinson Bianchi (Houghton Mifflin, 1932).

In reprinting Thomas H. Johnson's text I have kept precisely to his readings, as well as to his line-arrangements, which are derived from the MSS. Responsibility for the punctuation is, however, my own. The use of capital letters, italics and quotation-marks in the MSS. is capricious and arbitrary, as is the use of other punctuation marks, especially the dash: this is used so freely and with so little apparent significance that it can be of interest only to textual scholars; to the general reader it is a serious distraction. It is not uncommon to find every phrase in a sentence followed by a dash. The MS reading. of the first stanza of No. 32, for instance, is as follows:

> "Heaven"—is what I cannot reach!
> The Apple on the Tree—
> Provided it do hopeless—hang—
> That—"Heaven" is—to Me!

'Quite properly', Mr. Johnson writes in his Introduction, 'such punctuation can be omitted in later editions, and the spelling and capitalization regularized, as surely she would have expected had her poems been published in her lifetime'. As regards the spelling, this has been regularized (but not anglicized) in the present edition, except in a few instances where the retention of the original appears to preserve some local flavour. To punctuate Emily Dickinson's poems involves decisions about their meaning, as previous editors have discovered; unfortunately, with poems which are sometimes highly cryptic, there is no guarantee against occasional misinterpretation.

J. R.

INTRODUCTION

I

Mr. Higginson,—Are you too deeply occupied to say if my verse is alive?

The mind is so near itself it cannot see distinctly, and I have none to ask.

Should you think it breathed, and had you the leisure to tell me, I should feel quick gratitude.

If I make the mistake, that you dared to tell me would give me sincerer honor toward you.

I enclose my name, asking you, if you please, sir, to tell me what is true?

That you will not betray me it is needless to ask, since honor is its own pawn.

WITH this letter, dated April 16, 1862, Emily Dickinson introduced herself and her poems to Thomas Wentworth Higginson. She was thirty-one years old, the unmarried daughter of a lawyer in Amherst, which was then, as it is now, a quiet academic village in the farming district of Massachusetts, a hundred miles west of Boston. She had lived there obscurely all her life. At the time she wrote to Higginson she had composed a considerable number of short poems—perhaps as many as three hundred—of which only three had hitherto appeared in print.[1] Most of her poems had been written within the preceding two or three years. Conscious of her growing powers, she now made her first and only attempt to gain wider recognition— or at least whatever assurance was to be had from testing her achievement by the judgement of the literary world.

[1] Only seven of her poems were printed during her lifetime, none in the form which she wrote them.

Higginson, a married man nearing forty years of age, had recently resigned from the Unitarian ministry to devote himself to liberal propaganda and literary journalism. In the April number of *The Atlantic Monthly* he had written a 'Letter to a Young Contributor', which offered encouragement and advice to unknown writers. His letters to her do not survive, but it appears that his reply was highly critical of the poems she sent, but interested and encouraging. On April 26 she wrote:

Mr. Higginson,—Your kindness claimed earlier gratitude, but I was ill, and write to-day from my pillow.

Thank you for the surgery; it was not so painful as I supposed. I bring you others, as you ask, though they might not differ. While my thought is undressed, I can make the distinction; but when I put them in the gown, they look alike and numb.

You ask how old I was? I made no verse, but one or two, until this winter, sir.

I had a terror since September, I could tell to none; and so I sing, as the boy does of the burying ground, because I am afraid.

You inquire my books. For poets, I have Keats, and Mr. and Mrs. Browning. For prose, Mr. Ruskin, Sir Thomas Browne, and the 'Revelations'! I went to school, but in your manner of the phrase had no education. When a little girl, I had a friend who taught me Immortality; but venturing too near, himself, he never returned. Soon after my tutor died, and for several years my lexicon was my only companion. Then I found one more, but he was not contented I be his scholar, so he left the land.

You ask of my companions. Hills, sir, and the sundown, and a dog large as myself, that my father bought me. They are better than beings because they know, but do not tell; and the noise in the pool at noon excels my piano.

I have a brother and sister; my mother does not care for thought; and father, too busy with his briefs to notice what we do. He buys me many books, but begs me not to read them, because he fears they joggle the mind. They are religious, except me, and address an eclipse, every morning, whom they call their 'Father'.

But I fear my story fatigues you. I would like to learn. Could you tell me how to grow, or is it unconveyed, like melody or witchcraft?

You speak of Mr. Whitman. I never read his book, but was told that it was disgraceful.

I read Miss Prescott's 'Circumstance', but it followed me in the dark, so I avoided her.

Two editors of journals came to my father's house this winter, and asked me for my mind, and when I asked them 'why' they said I was penurious, and they would use it for the world.

I could not weigh myself, myself. My size felt small to me. I read your chapters in the 'Atlantic', and experienced honor for you. I was sure you would not reject a confiding question.

Is this, sir, what you asked me to tell you?

Your friend,
E. Dickinson

Two explanatory notes to this letter may be given here. The 'terror' of which she writes must have been the devastating prospect of losing the only man she ever fully loved, Charles Wadsworth, of whom more will be said later. She did in fact lose him in the spring of 1862; this was the crisis of her life, and it precipitated her decision to seek the help and advice of Higginson. The 'friend who taught me Immortality' was a young man, Benjamin Newton, whom she had known in her 'teens and who had had much influence in forming her mind. He had died of tuberculosis in 1853. Most decisively of all, he had believed in her future as a poet. This belief she came, herself, quietly to share; she continued to send selections of her poems to Higginson and to receive his criticisms submissively, in the rôle of pupil acknowledging preceptor. Although Higginson evidently praised her work, he never understood it, and it soon became clear to her that he had no essential sympathy with her poetic aims. Over the gulf of separation between an original creator and his potential audience her poems had not spoken to Higginson with that clear immediacy, that instinctive sense of affinity, which are the conditions of real understanding. She knew (though she would never have so expressed it) that her poems were good; she hoped to have this knowledge confirmed by a man of the world; and she soon found out that her chosen mentor had no notion of what she was after. In June she wrote and thanked him for his praise, but quietly and gently rejected his professional advice—which must have been in the direction of regularizing and conventionalizing those qualities in her verse which made it unique. 'I smile (she added) when you suggest that I delay "to publish", that being foreign to my thought as firmament to fin. If fame belonged to me, I could not escape her; if she did not, the longest day would pass me on the chase, and the approbation of my dog would forsake me then. My barefoot rank is better'.

She proves of course more than her rectitude—her rightness. The pursuit of fame is ignoble: pursuit is not the function of men but of dogs, who have the right to despise their masters if they engage in it. The letter concludes with a half-protest against Higginson's strictures on her verse technique, and an almost piteous appeal for his continued encouragement and for advice which implicitly she rejects in advance. It is a curious letter, firm in intention yet confused in feeling. The confusion comes from her not having so far realized just what it was she wanted when she wrote to Higginson. Most of her life was an inner and spiritual one, and we are forced to guess at her feelings; for there was always a note of reserve about even her most confessional writing. She disliked self-revelation for its own sake.

> The reticent volcano keeps
> His never slumbering plan;
> Confided are his projects pink
> To no precarious man.
>
> If nature will not tell the tale
> Jehovah told to her,
> Can human nature not survive
> Without a listener?
>
> Admonished by her buckled lips
> Let every babbler be;
> The only secret people keep
> Is immortality.

It is certain that at times she craved, if not fame, at any rate some measure of recognition during her lifetime. One of her editors[1] goes so far as to say:

> Because Emily Dickinson refused to publish, it has been assumed that she did not care for fame. By way of evidence to the contrary, poems found among these latest scraps prove that she was obsessed by the thought of it. Indeed, she was so conscious that she deserved it that she had to keep continually reminding herself of its futility— that her own approval was all that mattered.

All creative artists need recognition and, according to their nature, strive consciously for it or adopt an attitude of indifference. Emily[2] refused to compromise her private standards of poetic method in order to satisfy the demands of literary convention as personified by Higginson. This is not to say she was more a martyr than any other pioneer: she could not have written Higginson's kind of verse even if she had wanted to. Her poems had faults, but these were not the faults that Higginson could have amended. They needed rigorous selection, but not at this stage. He did in fact prove himself later more successful at selection than at emendation. Possibly Emily's public was not yet born. Yet less than thirty years after she began her correspondence with Higginson the first posthumous collection of her poems, which with great hesitancy and misgivings he helped to put on the market, was a popular success. It is impossible to believe that some of these readers would not have appreciated a volume of her poems during her lifetime. She did of course refuse to publish; but this was not until it had been made clear to her that nothing would be published in a form she could approve. It is useless to guess what happiness and consolation would have been added to her later years if Higginson had sponsored publication in the 'sixties or 'seventies: one

---

[1] Millicent Todd Bingham: Introduction to *Bolts of Melody* (1945).

[2] I have adopted the not entirely satisfactory expedient of referring to Emily Dickinson by her christian name, since to use the whole name is sometimes cumbersome, and to use only the surname, as some critics do, seems somehow inappropriate.

can only hope that her assurance of the fame due to her at some date was never seriously shaken.

We are entitled to say that Higginson was a fool. Even so, it is difficult to say who at that time could have been found with the necessary judgement to accept Emily's poems as they were. A curious parallel is offered by the almost contemporary case of Hopkins and Bridges in England. Like Higginson, Bridges was not insensitive to the striking and original character of his friend's poems; like him, he was convinced that it was unwise to publish. In both cases it seems as if the sponsor were unwilling to risk his own professional standing, since his pupil had nothing to lose. Higginson and Bridges were both creative writers of a low order, earning their reputation along cautiously forward-looking paths. Both were well-meaning men who could neither actually repel the genius that came to them for help nor give it the full recognition which would have called in question their own mediocrity. There is perhaps necessarily a basic moral deficiency in inferior talents which are not content to accept inferior status; so that there was perhaps, in both Bridges and Higginson, a suppressed hatred for the work of their pupils, arising from unacknowledged jealousy. By contrast one thinks of Haydn and Mozart—of how the older composer's character is ennobled, as his music certainly loses nothing, by his un-stinted proclamation of his junior's superiority. In any case, both Emily and Hopkins were lonely and had need of en-couragement and an exchange of views with a professional writer. Friendship, though at first she did not know it, was what Emily needed, and got from Higginson.

She accepted the relationship. For the rest of her life she carried on an intermittent correspondence with him. sending him her poems and receiving his books and articles. She enjoyed the rôle of 'scholar', and he was gratified to be accepted as the preceptor of one he referred to as 'my eccentric poetess'. He was almost her only contact with the literary world. Her letters to him are gay, affectionate and sometimes revealing.

She had a warm regard for his interest in her, his good sense, his reliability as a man of the world. She later referred to him as 'my safest friend'.

It may seem odd that the two only met twice—once in 1870 and once in 1873. No one ever had greater need for human affection and sympathy than Emily, and no one was ever shyer. But about the time she first wrote to Higginson she began also to adopt the life of a recluse which became more and more her settled habit. After their first meeting Higginson wrote to his wife: 'I never was with anyone who drained my nerve power so much. Without touching her she drew from me. I am glad not to live near her'. Yet it was she who had urged the meeting, anticipating it with the utmost felicity and referring to it afterwards as an unforgettable joy. 'Of our greatest acts we are ignorant', she had written to him before the meeting. 'You were not aware that you saved my life'. She refers of course to the crisis in her affairs when she had appealed to Higginson ostensibly for literary advice but, under the surface, for comfort and assurance. When Higginson accepted the invitation, she wrote: 'The incredible never surprises me, because it is the incredible.' After the visit she wrote: 'Enough is so vast a sweetness, I suppose it never occurs, only pathetic counterfeits.'

Four years after Emily's death Higginson was persuaded to use his influence in getting a first selection of her poems published. He and Mabel Loomis Todd, the friend to whom Emily's papers had first been entrusted, did what they could to edit a number of the poems in such a way as to make them conform to conventional standards; they regularized the grammar, tidied up the rhymes and metrical oddities, and gave each poem a title of their own devising. Higginson did all he could to soften what he imagined would be the inevitable shock to public taste. The reviewers were on the whole hostile, but the reading public liked the poems, and new impressions were called for immediately. Emboldened by this unexpected success, Higginson and Mrs. Todd followed up this 1890 volume with two further volumes of poems and one of letters.

It was not until the 1920's, when further selections of the poems began to appear, that Emily Dickinson's long awaited fame was securely established. In the intellectual climate of those years she could be appreciated for what she was—one of the greatest of American poets, and perhaps the greatest woman poet who had ever lived. It was discovered that the number of poems and fragments she had left was enormous, and further selections, less drastically emended, appeared during the second quarter of this century. In 1937 appeared a comprehensive collection, and this was repeatedly reprinted during the succeeding years. It was not, however, until very recently that the whole body of her poems received the attention of a professional textual scholar. At last, in 1955, Mr. Thomas H. Johnson's definitive edition in three volumes was published by the Harvard University Press. This supersedes all previous editions and corrects many inaccuracies and misreadings in the hitherto accepted texts. It is possible now, therefore, to form a reliable judgement, based on all the existing evidence, of Emily Dickinson's poetry. It is the main purpose of the present selection to do a little towards persuading readers to accept her poems for what they are—not simply an outstanding manifestation of American genius, but as *English* poems worthy of a place in whatever is variously regarded—according to the critical judgement of succeeding periods—as 'the canon'. In one sense all poetry that has any value is local, both in place and time. Chaucer was a fourteenth century Londoner, Hardy a nineteenth century west-countryman, Wordsworth a northerner, Dunbar a Scot, Emily Dickinson a New Englander. All spoke English, and to a lesser degree all wrote it, with a local accent. But the language they thought and felt and composed in was one language. If English readers have accustomed themselves to think of those others simply as poets, it seems to me fully time to drop the qualification 'American' and regard Emily Dickinson simply as a poet, while in no way denying, but rather confirming, the honour which belongs to America for having given her a birthplace.

II

In fact, although New England gave Emily her local habitation, it was old England which gave her her name. In 1630, just two centuries before Emily's birth, Nathaniel Dickinson of Ely, in the county of Cambridge, sailed for America in search of independence and religious freedom.

Amherst, where the Dickinsons settled, was a small agricultural township. Such communities, of which New England was composed until the rise of the manufacturing towns in the nineteenth century, were theocratic to an extent difficult to realize in England. The church and its management was the centre of life, and the standards of thought and conduct were those of Calvinistic puritanism.[1] Life was narrow, and social and political ideas were rigid; the gospel of prosperity through hard work and self-denial made severe demands on the individual; but it did not stamp out individuality, and it encouraged self-respect and neighbourly kindness. If thrift and good housekeeping claimed most of the attention of the women, and hard work and self-improvement the efforts of the men, there was room for a vigorous mental life and the satisfaction of intellectual curiosity for any whose bent was in that direction. The impression one gains from the correspondence of Emily and her friends is of a life free from triviality, serious in purpose,

[1] In his excellent biographical account of Emily Dickinson, *This was a Poet* (New York, 1938) George F. Whicher speaks of the 'current of evangelistic humanitarian piety' which flowed through New England life in the early nineteenth century, to an extent almost incredible to the modern reader.

but with scope for gaiety and the lively exchange of ideas; there is no sense of repression or of the gloom usually associated with puritanism.

Emily's grandfather, Samuel Fowler Dickinson, was one of the founders of Amherst College, an institution of higher education dedicated mainly to the training of men for the ministry; her father, Edward Dickinson, became one of the principal citizens and for many years the bursar of the college. He was a lawyer by profession, stern, reserved, generous, and public-spirited. Emily Norcross, whom he married in 1828, appears to have been a nonentity, quiet, submissive, and domesticated. The Dickinson household was patriarchal, and it is evident that Emily adored her father, though not un-critically. Her elder brother Austin was a gentle, sensitive man, the shadow of his father. He married in 1856 an Amherst girl, Susan Gilbert, already a close friend of Emily's, having in common with her a lively interest in literature. They and their children remained lifelong neighbours of the elder Dickinsons, with whom Emily lived all her life; so that the small inner circle of Emily's intimates, though occasionally strained, was never broken. The circle was completed by the younger sister, Lavinia Dickinson, who, like Emily, never married. She was devoted to her sister and became, during the years of Emily's seclusion, almost her only link with the outside world. Lavinia knew that Emily wrote poems, but her surprise at the immense number of them which came to light on Emily's death was genuine. It was Lavinia who took the first steps towards making her sister's work more widely known. She became something of the proverbial spinster, and in later life Emily referred affectionately to Lavinia's 'pussies and posies'. Immediately outside the family circle, which was held tight by mutual respect for the differing personalities of its members, was a larger circle of aunts, uncles, and cousins, and of school friends and neighbours with whom the Dickinsons were on terms of affectionate intimacy. College and church provided the intellectual and social centre of Amherst life; Edward Dickinson was closely associated with both, so that his pleasant and spacious house in Main Street became a meeting place for much eager and animated social intercourse.

Emily's health was at times delicate, more owing to high nervous tension than to any constitutional weakness. Trouble with her eyes led to prolonged visits to Boston in middle life, but apart from the nervous collapse which occurred two years before her death she suffered no serious illness. When young she was sociable and earned some admiration for her wit and high spirits. Her letters during her girlhood are full of self-conscious exuberance, shrewd observation, and sentimental professions of friendship. Her schooling was perhaps not so ineffectual as she implied later when writing to Higginson. She experienced eight years of irregular schooling, first at Amherst Academy and then at Mount Holyoke Female Seminary, between the ages of eleven and eighteen. She succeeded well enough in the typical curriculum of the day, but she learned more, as was the custom with young ladies at that time, from her friendships both with contemporaries and with older men and women, and from her reading. It was her friends who awakened her mind to the world of books and ideas beyond the narrow paths of puritan theology and devotion. Yet she was never, like Elizabeth Barrett, a bluestocking, ardent in the pursuit of learning for its own sake. 'Miss Dickinson was a recluse,' writes Allen Tate[1]; 'but her poetry is rich with a profound and varied experience.' It is one of the mysteries about Emily Dickinson, this apparent discrepancy between the sources of her knowledge and its depth and extent. No doubt her knowledge came from observation, experience, and suffering, against a background of unsystematic but deeply assimilated reading, behind all of which lay a tenacious hold on the puritan doctrine inherited from the tradition in which she and her ancestors had been brought up. She must have forgotten little

[1] *On the Limits of Poetry*, New York, 1948.

of what she heard and read. One has the impression, reading the mass of her poems, that nothing that went into her mind was wasted. We have no records of a mind so rich in knowledge and so devoid of lumber.

Her position with regard to the all-pervasive puritan theology of her environment is not easy to define. She attended church, but she never joined it as a full member; her inner ear was tuned to the accents of the service and its hymns, to the language of the Bible, and the fathers of Calvinist doctrine. The only undeniable stylistic influence on her poetry was the language, and especially the metres, of the hymns she heard at church. Yet she remained always critical of the assumptions about God, Heaven, and the human soul on which the traditional doctrine was based. Of this doctrine Allen Tate says: 'It gave . . . an heroic proportion and a tragic mode to the experience of the individual'—and again: 'Socially we may not like the New England idea. Yet it had an immense, incalculable value for literature: it dramatised the human soul.'

Too much effort has been expended on trying to account for Emily's unique and isolated genius. American writers have been at pains to show how 'the New England tradition' can be invoked to explain her emergence; yet the story of her family is that of countless other families which did not happen to produce poets. Nevertheless, though nothing will ever explain how Emily Dickinson came to be a poet, this idea of the drama of sin and redemption goes some way towards accounting for the intensely dramatic impression left by the poems of one whose outer life was so conspicuously lacking in drama.

Her brief poems are full of intense, even violent, instants— instants which seem to contain within themselves epochs of feeling. But the drama is always inward and spiritual, not outward and sensational.

My life closed twice before its close

About such a statement there is that which precludes the

possibility of mere invention; it strikes us as being made, not of words, but of life.

After her formal education was finished, Emily settled down in her parents' home to enact the inner drama of her existence. The ten years which follow are singularly lacking in documentation. Her letters describe a life given up to the domestic routine, to everyday interests, and to occasional visits to relatives and friends. So sparsely indeed is the whole of her life documented that her biography is largely a matter of inference. Among her poems are many of the kind usually called love poems, though none of them are in any sense 'usual' poems. They are at times passionate, though rarely is there any indication of physical passion. Nevertheless, any reader examining the poems without external biographical knowledge gains the impression of a single all-mastering love frozen, as it were, in the moment of ecstasy by a supreme act of renunciation. Something like this was in fact the central event of Emily's life; but just how far it was actualized is still not clear. In the fifty years after her death speculations of the most sensational kind were indulged in. All that her most recent biographers will assert as fact is that the object of her single passion was the Rev. Charles Wadsworth, a preacher in Philadelphia whom she heard and perhaps visited in 1854. Wadsworth was evidently a fine preacher, possessed of a certain intellectual and spiritual magnetism. He was a rigid and conventional Calvinist in outlook, though in no way lacking in kindness and humanity. He was forty years old, happily married, and with a family. He corresponded with Emily, but none of their letters survive. It seems extremely unlikely that Emily could have been given any encouragement in her hopeless and consuming passion, nor could she have imagined for it anything but a tragic future. It may be that the relationship she traces in her poems had no basis whatever except on a purely imaginative plane. It is on that plane alone that we need read the poems of passion; though we must not make the mistake of supposing that the passion was any the less real or intense on that account. We know much of Emily Dickinson on the human plane—much more than we are ever likely to know of Shakespeare. But we must accept the Emily of the poems as the real woman, as we accept the Shakespeare of the sonnets and the plays as the real Shakespeare. Between the actual, everyday person—the person known to the recipients of her familiar letters and those who caught glimpses of her in Amherst or left brief records of interviews—between the actual person and the writer of the poems there is a gulf which no amount of documentation, however interesting it might be, could span. Much as we should like to know more of the actual Shakespeare, who can suppose that any factual evidence which might come to light would not, in his case too, leave the gulf unspanned?

The remaining known facts of the relationship are these: Wadsworth seems to have called on Emily twice—once in 1860 and again twenty years later; in the spring of 1862 he left Philadelphia, where he was comparatively near Emily, and accepted a call to become pastor of Calvary Church in San Francisco, on the other side of the American continent. Whatever the outward facts of the situation, this was, in the inner drama of Emily's existence, death. It had been preceded by an agonized renunciation. It was once believed that Wadsworth had proposed an elopement and that Emily had refused to ruin another woman's life. There is no evidence whatever for this. Yet readers will always wonder what exactly it was that Emily renounced. In the absence of other facts, which are most unlikely to materialize, they will have to fall back on the idea of a purely imaginative self-denial. There is nothing improbable in this; nor need the impact of the poems of renunciation be weakened. I believe that Emily may have come to regard herself as not destined for marriage, and even as not being attractive to the opposite sex.[1] The references to herself in an apologetic vein occur throughout her poems. She admits to being 'freckled', and more than once uses this word in the sense of 'blemished'. In the lines beginning *He touched me, so I live to know* she speaks of 'My gipsy face transfigured'; in *A prison gets to be a friend* she speaks of 'Our escapeless features' (though not necessarily in a disparaging sense). A poem written about 1862, describing in circumstantial detail a visit by an unnamed 'he' and her reception of him, begins:

> Again his voice is at the door.
> I feel the old degree.
> I hear him ask the servant
> For such an one as me.
>
> I take a flower as I go,
> My face to justify.
> He never saw me in this life—
> I might surprise his eye!

In the MS. there is a suggested change from 'surprise' to 'not please' in the last line. This practice of greeting callers with a flower in her hand became habitual with her. Somewhere, deep down in her nature, there was a basis of fear—a fear which in her poems she overcame: perhaps, psychologically, this was their purpose. Her constitutional timidity may have been connected with a profound sense of personal unacceptability.[2]

[1] Describing twenty years later his visit to Emily in 1870 when she was nearly forty, Higginson referred to her as 'a plain shy little person, the face without a single good feature. . . . She had a quaint and nunlike look'. (Article in *The Atlantic Monthly*, October 1891.) Other observers were less unflattering. Most agreed on the beauty of her auburn hair, which was naturally curly but which the puritan fashion obliged her to force into uncompromising straightness. Her niece, Martha Dickinson Bianchi (*Emily Dickinson Face to Face*, Boston 1932) writes of her dark eyes, Titian hair, white skin, and the deep low voice which many found attractive.

[2] She had learned it also at her father's knee. There was fear as well as adoration in her attitude to him. She told Higginson that she had not learned to tell the time until she was fifteen because she dared not confess that she had not understood his explanation; she could not ask anyone else for fear he found out.

She became almost pathologically incapable of undergoing personal interviews: it was as if her true element was correspondence rather than personal contact. Not that there was any deficiency of normal sexuality. Her earliest known poem, written when she was twenty, was a sentimental, playfully amorous valentine addressed to a young man in her father's office. It is in the style of the time, but it is worth noting that this contains the first of innumerable lines concerned with bees and their fertilizing function:

> The bee doth court the flower, the flower his suit receives,
> And they make merry wedding, whose guests are hundred leaves

She showed a significant unwillingness to grow up, and this was no doubt part of her timidity, for which she so conspicuously compensates in her poems. It seems probable that in her 'twenties her shrinking from 'life' on the plane of physical actuality became acute; possibly the shock of finding herself irredeemably committed to an unattainable love proved decisive. It may have confirmed her in her readiness to accept a passive rôle so far as external action was concerned. Nothing, then, would be more probable than that she should dramatize her situation on the imaginative plane as an agonized renunciation. Nothing would be shallower than to suppose this renunciation to be any the less real. The renunciation of a hope, however irrational, may be no less heroic than the renunciation of an actual possession.

On the departure of Wadsworth to San Francisco Emily immediately sought the professional advice of Higginson about her poems. The results have been described. Nothing would be easier than to elaborate the hypothesis of a frustrated romance, succeeded by a retreat into the consolations and compensations of poetry. Such a hypothesis would be strengthened by the evidence of her deepening seclusion and withdrawal from the world. But this was not the case.

Her almost secret knowledge of herself as a poet went back

at least a decade, although her poetic output was not large until her late 'twenties. She began, as early as 1858, to make fair copies of her poems and to assemble them in the packets in which they were found after her death. In short, she had begun to accept the fact of a poetic destiny long before the crisis in her emotional life. It was the realization of her final commitment to a hopeless passion which quickened and intensified her poetic powers, which achieved their full magnitude during the years immediately following the crisis. In 1862 she wrote 366 poems (rather more than she had written in all the years before); in 1863 she wrote 141; in 1864, 174; and in 1865, 85. Thereafter, until the year of her death, her annual output varied between ten and fifty poems. It is a curious fact that the years of Emily Dickinson's greatest poetic productivity were exactly those of the American Civil War (1861-1865). The correlation between national upheaval and poetic fertility has often been noticed, and it is strange that this should operate in the case of a poet so exclusively concerned with the inner life and so apparently unconcerned with the war as Emily. That her own crisis coincided with the national crisis was accidental. But she dwelt in no ivory tower, and certainly was in no way unaffected by the quickening of national sensibility which occurred everywhere during the Civil War. Writing to her cousins about the death and burial of the first Amherst casualty, she says:

> sorrow seems more general than it did, and not the estate of a few persons, since the war began; and if the anguish of others helped one with one's own, now would be many medicines. 'Tis dangerous to value, for only the precious can alarm. I noticed that Robert Browning had made another poem, and was astonished—till I remembered that I, myself, in my smaller way, sang off charnel steps. Every day life feels mightier, and what we have the power to be, more stupendous.

The reference to Browning concerns the death of his wife in 1861. Browning's devotion to her was famous, and Emily was an admirer of her poems. Emily had her own anxieties, and Higginson's personal danger as a colonel in the Union Army on active service caused her continual alarm.

Higginson's epithets 'quaint and nunlike' in his reminiscences of Emily have had unfortunate consequences. She has been repeatedly called 'the nun of Amherst', and this is misleading. A nun is a member of a religious sisterhood, Emily's withdrawal was from all human community except that of her family. She withdrew for many reasons, but a broken heart was not one of them. Conrad Aiken's word 'hermit' is nearer the truth: 'It is apparent that Miss Dickinson became a hermit by deliberate and conscious choice.'[1]

She had dedicated herself to poetry and was becoming daily more aware of the growing power pressing in her for utterance. That she took to dressing in white and refused to see callers except by proxy, through her sister, was part of the drama she played as a setting for her inner life. Legends of her eccentricity have been made much of, but in fact it was largely of a negative sort: it is not so much that she performed unconventional acts as that she refused to take part in convention. She remained in some degree childlike, not because of a psychopathic infantilism, but because the retention of innocence or naïveté was an essential condition of poetic integrity. She was not the only poet to maintain such a belief. Allen Tate remarks:

> All pity for Miss Dickinson's 'starved life' is misdirected. Her life was one of the richest and deepest ever lived on this continent. When she went upstairs and closed the door, she mastered life by rejecting it.

This is well said, if by 'life' we understand the conventional round of small-town preoccupations. But she did not reject life in its more permanent aspect; she withdrew in order to apprehend it more fully and with greater concentration of purpose. We need not, indeed, pity her 'starved life', but we may sympathise with her loneliness, which she overcame, not

[1] Introduction to *Selected Poems of Emily Dickinson*, London, 1924.

by indulging in self-pity, but by intellectualizing it in her characteristically paradoxical mode.

> It might be lonelier
> Without the loneliness

She did not withdraw from the world because she hated it: there was nothing in her of the grand romantic manner, rejecting society because the palate had become jaded. Her isolation was a calculated choice, the loss weighed against the gain, with a clear conviction of the necessity and worth of what she had to do. She had lived for thirty years in Amherst, learning what she could of the world, reading and thinking, and above all, drawing all the inspiration and comfort she could from the friendships she cultivated so lovingly. Once she had renounced marriage in the accepted sense and adopted the rôle of unacknowledged wife to a man nearly three thousand miles away, there was no new experience which the world could offer.

> The soul selects her own society,
> Then shuts the door.
> To her divine majority
> Present no more.
>
> Unmoved she notes the chariots pausing
> At her low gate;
> Unmoved, an Emperor be kneeling
> Upon her mat.
>
> I've known her from an ample nation
> Choose one,
> Then close the valves of her attention
> Like stone.

She chose to live each day out in the presence of all that thought, memory, letters, and the immensity of nature could give her, without any of the distractions of casual intercourse, or any of the alleviations it might offer from the ever-pressing burden of her own identity.

> Adventure most unto itself
> The soul condemned to be,
> Attended by a single hound,
> Its own identity.

When Higginson questioned her about her seclusion, she wrote:

> Of 'shunning men and women',—they talk of hallowed things, aloud, and embarrass my dog. He and I don't object to them, if they'll exist their side. I think Carlo would please you, he is dumb, and brave.

Those she selected for her friends were to her peculiarly alive; the rest she could scarcely understand. 'So few that live have life', she wrote to Samuel Bowles, one of her most cherished friends. And again to Higginson:

> I find ecstasy in living; the mere sense of living is joy enough. How do most people live without any thoughts? There are many people in the world,—you must have noticed them in the streets,—how do they live? How do they get strength to put on their clothes in the morning?

And again to Higginson:

> To live is so startling, it leaves but little room for other occupations, though friends are, if possible, an event more fair. . . . A letter always feels to me like Immortality because it is the mind alone without corporeal friend. . . . There seems a spectral power in thought that walks alone.

It was the quotidian sanity of the world around her which Emily found oppressive.

> Much madness is divinest sense
> To a discerning eye—
> Much sense the starkest madness.
> 'Tis the majority
> In this, as all, prevail.

> Assent and you are sane;
> Demur, you're straightway dangerous
> And handled with a chain.

Or, as she expressed it in a letter, 'Insanity to the sane seems so unnecessary'.

Passages such as these, which show the quality of her mind and life, could be quoted indefinitely. There is no affectation in them. Even the vulgarian Higginson, convinced as he was of Emily's eccentricity, insisted that her behaviour was perfectly natural. To her a friend was, literally, 'an event', as was the arrival of a letter. Sunrise, noon, and sunset were the day's acts. The mountains were enormous presences—

> The mountain sat upon the plain
> In his tremendous chair,
> His observation omnifold,
> His inquest everywhere.

The sea was a symbol of love, of death, and of eternity, which were all closely connected in her mind. 'I cannot see how eternity seems,' she wrote to her cousins on the death of her mother in 1882. 'It sweeps around me like a sea.' Over twenty years earlier she had written:

> Exultation is the going
> Of an inland soul to sea,
> Past the houses, past the headlands,
> Into deep eternity.

Night was an unknown fear, a fear never wholly overcome, however often her poems strove to master it.

> Presentiment is that long shadow on the lawn
> Indicative that suns go down.

Thunderstorms held for Emily the fascination of terror, and are the subject of several of her finest poems. In all these things she felt, as she expressed it, 'a nearness to tremendousness'.

The only social or civic event which recurs with frequency in her poems is a funeral. Her apparent obsession with the physical panoply of death on the one hand, and with death and immortality as an idea on the other, is obvious to any reader of her poems. It might seem morbid, or merely sensational, if we allowed ourselves to forget two things. Emily's vision of life was essentially childlike, and to a child there is something ultimately fascinating in a funeral. A poem such as *There's been a death in the opposite house* (No. 59) is almost shocking in the primitive starkness of its detail and its cool detachment of vision; there is also something primitive in the terrible euphemism for the undertaker—'the man of the appalling trade'[1] But the poem is the reverse of morbid: it is a triumphantly successful attempt to purge terror by re-living the experience poetically in all its vivid and shocking clarity. In a later poem on death, the wonderful *Safe in their alabaster chambers* (No. 29), compassion supersedes terror. The dead are safe in their graves, beyond the reach of the sun, while nature around them goes on indifferently, but the poet has pity.[2]

> Pipe the sweet birds in ignorant cadence—
> Ah, what sagacity perished here!

It is obvious that to anyone so intensely aware of mere life, so preoccupied with the wonder and ecstasy of simple existence, the complementary theme of death must be a major concern. No doubt the idea of death and of triumph over death through personal immortality, was a principal factor in the religious climate in which Emily Dickinson breathed; but to the childish vision also, a vision dazzled by the spectacle of life, death as the negation of life must have been of peculiar significance; again, she wrote of it to master it. 'I sing, as the

[1] This device is employed also in the work of another American poet, John Crowe Ransom, whose diction seems to have been influenced by that of Emily Dickinson. He refers, for instance, to a coffin as 'the box of death' (*Dead Boy*) and to a messenger about to take a fateful letter as 'the blue-capped functioner of doom' (*Parting, without a Sequel*).

[2] Compare a letter to her cousins on the death of a favourite aunt in 1860: 'The birds keep singing just the same. Oh! The thoughtless birds.'

boy does of the burying ground, because I am afraid.' But death, in this sense, could not be the end. Emily believed in immortality both as a religious dogma and as a poetic idea. She was prepared to adopt a childlike notion of Heaven in a quite literal and localised sense, but she refused to accept the notion of life as a vale of tears from which Heaven is the only refuge.[1] Earth, viewed properly, was Heaven; life, in its permanent aspect, was immortality. Immortality in her poems means variously transcendant joy, self-fulfilment, life purged of the temporal and accidental.

The importance of the grave is that it is the temporal resting-place between life and eternity.

> Ample make this bed;
> Make this bed with awe.
> In it wait till judgment break
> Excellent and fair.

Here we have the mention of another idea which, as Thomas H. Johnson points out,[2] is of central importance in Emily's thought. 'Awe' is fear divested of its physical attribute and raised to the status of a mental attitude. It is the spiritual form of fear, or the corporeal form of reverence; an intellectualized emotion peculiarly suited to Emily's temperament. Awe is the stable form of that fluid complex of feelings—surprise, wonder, ecstasy, fear—with which she looks at life and death.

In touching on some of the main themes of Emily Dickinson's poetry, and in relating them to the circumstances of her life, it may be thought that I have suggested a somewhat forbidding and austere personality. In trying to reveal the poet in the

[1] 'My only sketch, profile, of Heaven is a large, blue sky, bluer and larger than the *biggest* I have seen in June, and in it are my friends—all of them—every one of them—those who are with me now, and those who were "parted" as we walked, and "snatched up to Heaven". If roses had not faded, and frosts had never come, and one had not fallen here and there whom I could not waken, there were no need of other Heaven than the one below—and if God had been here this summer, and seen the things that *I* have seen—I guess that He would think His Paradise superfluous.' (*Letter to Mrs. Holland, late summer,* 1856.)

[2] *Emily Dickinson: An Interpretive Biography.* Harvard University Press, 1955.

woman, some such distortion is inevitable. Yet nothing could be less faithful to the facts.

Emily's letters and the reminiscences of her family and friends reveal a sweet and sensitive nature, almost defective in egotism. She is one of the most delightful and witty of letter writers, her correspondence being used mainly as a medium for her friendships. A typical expression of friendship occurs in a letter to Mrs. Holland, written about 1857:

> After you went, a low wind warbled through the house like a spacious bird, making it high but lonely. When you had gone the love came. I supposed it would. The supper of the heart is when the guest is gone. Shame is so intrinsic in a strong affection we must all experience Adam's reticence.

As she wrote to Samuel Bowles, 'My friends are my estate', and she cultivated them as she cultivated her garden, with love, and with a kind of instinctive understanding which is called, in gardeners, 'green fingers'. She was considered by men of the world somewhat 'uncanny' in her personal magnetism. Yet to those she knew well and felt at ease with she was witty and vivacious. Her letters are full of the riddling, aphoristic quality found in her poems. She was in all things a stylist, fastidious in language as in dress. To Mrs. Holland she wrote, in 1876:

> An unexpected impediment to my reply to your dear last, was a call from my Aunt Elizabeth—'the only male relative on the female side', and though many days since, its flavour of court-martial still sets my spirit tingling.

For each of her correspondents she had a different manner: the differences are in some cases slight, but they are enough to show her uncommon gift for sympathy with people of differing temperaments and interests. Her letters to Higginson are very dissimilar in tone and attitude to those she wrote her young cousins. To each of her friends she brought a peculiar gift of understanding and affection. Yet all her letters are unmistakably her own.

Friends were her estate, but language was her province, and she delighted in perfecting it, whether in verse or in prose. She had what can only be called an aristocratic spirit, high-minded but without a trace of priggishness, serious without self-importance, shrewd enough to be malicious had she wished, but too gentle and kind for malice. She could, and often did, write sentimentally; but she never sentimentalized over the avoidable weaknesses of the society around her. Her poems are sometimes satirical, and the commonest object of her criticism is religious hypocrisy.

> What soft cherubic creatures
> These gentlewomen are.
> One would as soon assault a plush
> Or violate a star.
>
> Such dimity convictions,
> A horror so refined
> Of freckled human nature,
> Of deity ashamed.

Emily could not be called misanthropic, yet she did not love people in the mass. She was too much a realist, too aristocratic, ever to have experienced that all-embracing love of humanity so loudly proclaimed by her contemporary, Walt Whitman. There was in her nature, not only the kind and gentle friend, the gay and tender benefactor of children, the acute observer of human foibles—there was also the lonely animal, the outcast, the prisoner.

> Civilization spurns the leopard.
> Was the leopard bold?
> Deserts never rebuked her satin,
> Ethiop her gold.
> Tawny her customs,
> She was conscious;
> Spotted her dun gown.
> This was the leopard's nature, Signor—
> Need a keeper frown?

> Pity the pard that left her Asia.
> Memories of palm
> Cannot be stifled with narcotic
> Nor suppressed with balm.

There is here a certain savagery, almost a savagery of despair. For it cannot be doubted that the poem is autobiographical; and it is tempting with this, as with so many of her poems, to say that it represents her last word on life. But the more one reads her best poems, the more one sees that it is as idle with her as it is with Shakespeare to take any single quotation from her work and say that this is her last word. In a sense, everything she said was final. It is noticeable that amongst the published criticism of her work little agreement is to be found as to which are her finest poems. The fact is that, viewed as a whole, they have the quality of universality; in the realm of personal emotion there is very little, even sexual passion, which she does not touch on. She lived, in effect, in a single room; but the universe of her poems is immense. There are few poets, if any, who can suggest such large areas of proved emotion and experience in so few words. It was because she felt compelled to experience 'a nearness to tremendousness' that she had to withdraw from whatever was parochial. Her universe was bounded by infinite horizons, presided over by dawns, sunsets and mountains, clothed with trees and flowers, inhabited by birds, beasts and insects; yet it was not the Romantic world of pantheistic nature in which man was an intruder. On the contrary, Nature in itself was destructive; it meant, in the end, death. Without human sensibility, and the inter-dependence of man and man through love, the universe was meaningless. Immortality, the triumph over nature, was more than a religious dogma, it was a fact of daily life. Heaven and earth were co-extensive, and Emily believed fervently in both. Her Eternity is an eternity of space rather than of time; time appears comparatively little in her poetry; but space is her constant concern.

Great streets of silence led away
To neighborhoods of pause.
Here was no notice, no dissent,
No universe, no laws.

By clocks 'twas morning, and for night
The bells at distance called,
But epoch had no basis here
For period exhaled.

This is typical of the child's vision, which is spatial rather than temporal. The apprehension of space is the beginning of growth; the apprehension of time is the beginning of death. In Hardy, on the other hand, whom Emily resembles in some things, especially in her preoccupation with death, the sense of time is always insistent.

The childlike element in Emily's poetry has perhaps been one of the chief causes why full appreciation has been withheld, and why even enthusiastic criticism contains a note of reservation. Her faults have had too great an influence on her detractors, as her unique life has had too great an influence on her admirers. We live in an age of sophistication where everything is tolerated in poetry except what is called 'lack of technique'. 'She had genius but no technique' is the substance of a criticism often made. But it seems to me that the positive qualities of Emily's poetry entitle it to a place among the best, even though sophistication prevents official criticism from acknowledging it. She was a major poet, if that term has any meaning.[1] She dwelt

[1] It would be hard, for instance, to deny to Emily Dickinson her majority on the basis of the criteria suggested in T. S. Eliot's essay 'What is Minor Poetry?' (*On Poetry and Poets*, London, 1957.) Eliot desiderates 'significant unity' in the work of a major poet. Again, 'the difference between major and minor poets has nothing to do with whether they wrote long poems, or only short poems . . .'; and Eliot instances the lyrics of Blake and the shorter poems of Donne. Nor does he insist that the greater part of a major poet's work must be good, only that it requires to be read. Despite the uneven quality of Emily's poems, and the practical necessity for the general reader to study them in selection, I believe that the significance of even the best of them is greatly enhanced by a reading of the whole.

at large on the major themes of love, life, death and eternity; she was a wholly dedicated and fulfilled poet, achieving over a considerable extent of time a considerable number of successes in the control and use of language. What is more important, in a significant number of poems language achieved control over her; when inspiration seized her, she had sufficient mastery over her medium to be able to surrender completely. No poet is continuously inspired for long periods; no poet can stand much of the madness which is 'divinest sense'. Emily Dickinson had the courage not only to devote her whole energy to working out her poetic destiny, but also to devise a way of living poetically, whatever deprivations it might entail.

The life which Emily had dedicated to poetry with such single-mindedness came to an end in May 1886. The cause of her death was Bright's disease. She was buried where she had been born and had passed almost all her life, in Amherst. Her final years were all but devoid of outward event. They were saddened by the deaths of those nearest her. In 1874 her father died, and a year later her mother was paralysed, but lived until 1882. Her sister, her brother and his wife, Sue, all survived her. The collecting, arranging, and editing of all her poems and letters, which began immediately after her death, was not definitively completed until 1958.

III

Emily Dickinson wrote 1,775 poems and fragments. Many of them are simply odd quatrains jotted down in evident incompleteness. The majority are short—not more than eight lines in hundreds of instances—and most of the longest run to only six or eight four-line stanzas. What has been forgotten by some critics is that she never certainly gave any of her poems a final form, never polished them for the press, never made a selection for publication, never had the occasion, as most poets have, to destroy her failures. She never had the benefit of competent professional guidance, and—what is worse for a poet—she lacked the friendship of fellow-craftsmen which would have afforded that free exchange of opinion and criticism, praise and censure, which alone affords a healthy climate for active poetic growth. As she said to Higginson, 'I have none to ask.' Her sister-in-law, Susan Gilbert, gave her the benefit of her enthusiasm over a long period; but in all the finer aspects of her creative life Emily worked in virtual isolation. Hopkins knew that Bridges could not understand his poetic aims and methods, but at least he could discuss them and argue about them. Emily had only her own judgement to consult. During the last decade of her life she could enjoy the admiration and friendship of another woman writer, Helen Hunt Jackson, who was always urging her to allow some of her poems to be published. But by then it was too late: Emily knew that publication meant emendation, and by this time she was so little interested in immediate recognition that she absolutely declined to publish. She had evidently been persuaded by Higginson that there was no public for her poems as they were, and on this decision she remained firm.

We have, then, the almost unique heritage of the entire output of a poet, finished as well as unfinished poems, working drafts, failures and all. A great many of Emily's poems and fragments would have been put in the fire by any poet selecting and editing his work for publication. Any poet's reputation would suffer from the scrutiny of every line he jotted down in the conditions in which Emily wrote. Yet critics have treated her entire output as if it were her considered 'works', and failures have been analysed, not as expendable waste-products of an extraordinarily fertile mind, but as equal in status to her acknowledged successes. Much of what Emily left would certainly not have been preserved by most poets—much of it would not even have been written down. The kind of failures we find are failures in the technique of expression, and failures in what can only be called aesthetic judgement—poems, that is, in which mere sentimental or whimsical fancies have been put into verse. Most poets are guilty of failures in aesthetic judgement or taste, but they are sensible enough not write them down, or —if they do—not to leave them among their papers. Every poet knows the experience of mistaking a sentimental impulse for real poetic emotion, and discovering his mistake in the process of composition. The muse can delude with false fire. Of these failures of Emily's, as with those of any other genuine poet, we can say that they were uninspired. Yet it would be as mistaken simply to dismiss them as to make too much of them. They should be treated as apprentice-work, sketches, exercises in sensibility such as most poets need to perform, even when they have achieved maturity. For

> every attempt
> Is a wholly new start, and a different kind of failure.

The following, written about 1878, is a fairly typical example of a bad poem:

> Go not too near a house of rose.
> The depredation of a breeze
> Or inundation of a dew
> Alarm its walls away.
> Nor try to tie the butterfly,
> Nor climb the bars of ecstasy.
> In insecurity to lie
> Is joy's insuring quality.

The theme of the poem is the well-worn idea that joy dissolves if we try to capture it, a discovery that we all have to make for ourselves. To express this idea by a warning not to go too near a rose for fear of shattering it, and not to 'tie' a butterfly—as if anyone would—is doomed to failure through sentimentality, if not absurdity. Yet this is not silliness, it is experiment; the failure is not exactly one of judgement, but rather of inspiration. If a poet were to continuously apply critical judgement, the best poems would never be written. About the greatest poetry there is often an element of absurdity, only the inspiration transcends the absurdity.

> Let no sunrise' yellow noise
> Interrupt this ground.

So Emily concludes a poem on the making of a grave (No. 116). This is, if anything, more absurd than the admonition not to tie the butterfly, but it is triumphantly justified by its context. All the timidity and shyness which Emily displayed in life were turned to audacity and bold invention in her poems. The risk attending such audacity is that the failure, when the muse is absent, is correspondingly conspicuous. Anyone who begins a poem 'I felt a funeral in my brain' is undertaking something which, if it fails, will turn to the most hopeless bathos:

> And then I heard them lift a box
> And creak across my soul
> With those same boots of lead again.
>
> (No. 40)

Bathos is avoided, because the poet is master of the situation or because the situation has mastery over the poet: it is the same thing. The result is a unique and daring statement of a condition of mind near to madness, realized with terrifying fidelity; a state of near-hysteria has been transmuted into a signally powerful poetic utterance. In short, the strength and the weakness of Emily's work are inseparably bound up together; only in no other poet is so much of the weakness so ruthlessly displayed.

In a curiously uneven book[1] the American critic R. P. Blackmur writes:

The final skill of a poet lies in his so conducting the work he does

---

[1] *Language as Gesture* (London, Allen and Unwin ; New York, Harcourt, Brace).

deliberately do, that the other work—the hidden work, the inspiration, the genius—becomes increasingly available not only in new poems but in old poems re-read.

Blackmur is not here discussing Emily Dickinson, and he continues:

> The only consistent exhibition of such skill in the last century is in the second half of the career of W. B. Yeats.

He is not expressly discussing Yeats: the quotation comes from an essay on Hardy, a poet with whom Blackmur is as much out of sympathy as he is with Emily. When he comes to write of her, he cannot apply his own excellent generalization to the sum of her work. The work Emily 'did deliberately'—the bathetic, contrived verses—was precisely the journeyman, apprentice work which made 'the hidden work' possible.

It is worth considering this critic's views on Emily in some detail, because, even where wrong, they are illuminating.[1] Blackmur makes a perfunctory admission of Emily's greatness, but most of his essay is concerned to deny it. He concedes that she had 'an aptitude for language' (a critical meiosis worthy of note) but objects that she was naïve and unprofessional.

'Success was by accident, by the mere momentum of sensibility. . . . Most of the Dickinson poems seem to have been initially as near automatic writing as may be. The bulk remained automatic, subject to correction and multiplication of detail.'

The point is, surely, that there was success—not whether it came by accident or by design. And who is to prove that the greatest poetry is not 'automatic writing, subject to correction'? There is of course here a question of fundamental poetic theory, which cannot now be discussed fully. Blackmur is of the school of Eliot and Auden, both of whom have expressed themselves as opposed to the idea of inspiration in poetry. He prefers poetry which is demonstrably a wrought and contrived work of

[1] It should be pointed out that the essay on Emily Dickinson was first published in America in 1937, when ill-considered enthusiasm for the poet was at its height.

art. If a poet, like a pavement-artist, can write 'All my own work' beside his productions, and add 'No outside help from the Muse', the Apollonian critic is satisfied. At least he knows where he is: he can analyse, assess, compare. Emily, on the other hand, like many others from Plato onwards, undoubtedly held the Dionysian view by which 'All my own work' could certainly be taken as a certificate of failure. To the Dionysian poet there is no such thing as automatic writing, success is never by accident—it is by design, not of the poet but of the source of his inspiration.

Another objection Blackmur makes against Emily is on the score of her imagery.

> The most conspicuous of all is the vocabulary of romance royalty, fairy-tale kings, queens and courts, and the general language of chivalry. Emily Dickinson was as fond as Shakespeare of words like *imperial, sovereign, dominion*, and the whole collection of terms for rank and degree. Probably she got them more from Scott and the Bible and the Hymnal than from Shakespeare. There is none of Shakespeare's specific and motivating sense of kings and princes as the focus of society, and none of his rhetoric of power; there is nothing tragic in Emily Dickinson's royal vocabulary.

One would have thought that any critic would admit a hierarchical system of social organization as permissible in a poet's world. Emily's life was contained within, but not bounded by, the parochial, theocratic society of a small New England town. From this society she withdrew.

> The show is not the show
> But they that go.
> Menagerie to me
> My neighbour be.

The life she constructed for herself within, yet apart from, that society was lived in the world of her poetry; and that world was built, like the world of the classical renaissance, on a hierarchical order, in which flowers, insects, birds, animals, inanimate nature, humanity and divinity had their appointed places. It does not matter whether the pattern of her royal hierarchy derives from the Bible, from Shakespeare, or from myth and legend. It is perfectly valid within its context. The King is usually her lost lover, husband, master; the Queen is herself. It is difficult to believe that anyone could deny the tragedy in Emily's royal vocabulary who had read *I dreaded that first robin so* (No. 54), with its poignant yet triumphant assumption of the rôle of 'Queen of Calvary'.

Summing up, Blackmur writes: 'We have a verse in great body that is part terror, part vision, part insight and observation, which must yet mostly be construed as a kind of *vers de société* of the soul—not in form or finish but in achievement.'

'Terror, vision, insight, observation'—an admirable summary of the content of much of the poetry; but what are we to make of a phrase like '*vers de société* of the soul', except that it is glib, and not even a half-truth? *Vers de société* is a form of currency passed between the members of a coherent social group; it implies a community of interest and outlook. The phrase has no relevance to the situation of Emily Dickinson.

And here is this critic's final judgement:

She was neither a professional poet nor an amateur; she was a private poet who wrote indefatigably as some women cook or knit. Her gift for words and the cultural predicament of her time drove her to poetry instead of antimacassars. Neither her personal education nor the habit of her society as she knew it ever gave her the least inkling that poetry is a rational and objective *art* and most so when the theme is self-expression. She came, as Mr. Tate says, at the right time for one kind of poetry, the poetry of sophisticated, eccentric vision. That is what makes her good—in a few poems and many passages representatively great. But she never undertook the great profession of controlling the means of objective expression. That is why the bulk of her verse is not representative but mere fragmentary indicative notation. The pity of it is that the document her whole work makes shows nothing so much as that she had the themes, the insight, the observation, and the capacity for honesty,

xlii

which had she only known how—or only known why—would have made the major instead of the minor fraction of her verse genuine poetry. But her dying society had no tradition by which to teach her the one lesson she did not know by instinct.

It is of course customary in some critical schools to explain the emergence of a poet in terms of 'cultural predicaments' and the like. It is more difficult to explain why mid-nineteenth century New England was not a nest of singing birds, and why many of Emily's contemporaries probably did in fact make antimacassars. Poetry may be a 'rational and objective art' to R. P. Blackmur, or Pope, or Boileau, or Virgil; but it was not so to Plato, or Homer, or Shelley, or Coleridge, or Emily Dickinson. One need not quarrel with 'objective', but that it is a rational art there are many who would deny. It seems to me that in the case of Emily Dickinson it was more of a rite—a rite of propitiation towards the destructive forces of nature, death on the one hand and human sensibility on the other, performed as a relief from fear and ecstasy. The best of the poems are each the resolution of a personal problem experienced while under the possession of an abnormal state of emotion. To call the means of this resolution a 'rational art' is to evade most of the disputed questions about poetic creation.

Essentially Blackmur is in agreement with Higginson as to the eccentricity and indiscipline of Emily's poetry. The charge that she was neither a professional, nor an amateur, but a private poet, if it means anything, must be taken as being in Emily's favour; but that 'she wrote indefatigably as some women cook' betrays an anti-feminine irritation not uncommon in this context. Emily did also cook—very expertly, we are told, and her cooking was in part a propitiation of her father, who would eat no bread but hers, and in part a contribution to the well-being of her circle. She cooked, one might say, as some men write *vers de société*. Her poems were inspired by an altogether different allegiance. A friend who is also a literary critic has suggested, not perhaps quite seriously, that 'woman poet' is a contradiction in terms; and Mrs. Aphra Behn wrote of 'the man in me, the poet'. But it must be insisted that 'poet' also, in the true sense of the word, is a contradiction in terms. The poets may in fact have been mostly men, but men are not naturally poets. The irrational rôle of poet may fall on a woman at birth as on a man. The poetic elements in, say, *Mansfield Park* or *Wuthering Heights* are a proof of this.

There may indeed be something in the feminine habit of mind which, given the right conditions, would be especially favourable to the writing of a particular kind of poetry—though not necessarily to any kind that can be called a 'rational art'. Allen Tate, a critic of fine perceptions, is referring, I think, without realizing it, to the feminine habit of mind when he says:

> She could not in the proper sense think at all, and unless we prefer the feeble poetry of moral ideas that flourished in New England in the eighties, we must conclude that her intellectual deficiency contributed at least negatively to her great distinction.

What Tate means is that Emily could not rationalize in the masculine way. We are not aware of intellectual deficiency in her poems, as we are aware of poetic deficiency in Elizabeth Barrett's. The latter, educated in a strenuously male discipline, tried to reason like a man. Emily reasoned, or argued, in riddles and paradoxes:

> It might be lonelier
> Without the loneliness

and

> Water is taught by thirst

and

> The thought is quiet as a flake,
> A crash without a sound,
> How life's reverberation
> Its explanation found.

It is impossible to regard such lines as intellectually deficient. To express them in rational form would not be difficult, but it would be wasteful of words. Nor is such paradox a merely wilful display of wit; it is an essential part of Emily's mode of expression. Her wit has been compared to the metaphysical style of Donne; it may also be compared with the gnomic style of Blake. It occurs in her letters and was, according to witnesses, a feature of her conversation. I doubt if she was ever merely clever, or riddled simply for effect. She riddled for truth which, as she said, 'is such a rare thing. It is delightful to tell it.' But it is sometimes embarrassing, especially amidst the minor dishonesties demanded by social convention. Emily's reply to Higginson at the end of their first interview, when he said he would come again 'some time', punctured his little dishonesty without hurting him; perhaps at the time he did not even know what she meant: 'say, in a long time; that will be nearer. Some time is no time.'

Emily's arrival at the truth in this sibylline fashion is not so much irrational as super-rational. She was interested, not so much in a truth for its own sake—she was not a philosopher or a moralist—as in a direct vision of the truth. One might rationalize the vision or intuition after it had occurred, but that was not her business as a poet. In seeking to understand her poems, which are often highly cryptic, we require intuition rather than reason. In such a poem as *It dropped so low in my regard* Emily is indeed concerned with a moral observation, but she does not moralize.

> It dropped so low in my regard
> I heard it hit the ground
> And go to pieces on the stones
> At bottom of my mind;
>
> Yet blamed the fate that fractured less
> Than I reviled myself
> For entertaining plated wares
> Upon my silver shelf.

It is irrelevant to ask what 'it' is. The point of the poem is not to rebuke the 'it', whatever it is, for having appeared better than it was; it is, rather, to make the moral observation that when we have overestimated something, it is ourselves we blame for our initial lack of perception. An experience of self-reproach, such as this, had to be lived out, apprehended, and dismissed; it could not be dismissed until it had been given permanent embodiment in poetic form. Had Emily been primarily interested in moral observation, she would have written a prose treatise. But she was concerned with a different order of truth from the truth which is expressed in prose. If she was not a 'professional poet', she had no other profession. The technique of writing poems, not as a rational art, but as significant 'gesture' (to use Blackmur's word) was her constant pre-occupation. On the technical side—in so far as she is allowed to have had any technique at all—she has been censured for three faults: bad grammar, bad rhymes, and irregular rhythms. The grammar of her letters is conventional enough, and it must be supposed that the 'bad grammar' of the poems is deliberate, or at any rate justified in her eyes by the demands of poetic form. It may be that she regarded formal grammatical consistency as of less importance than compression and economy of language. Her use of a sort of subjunctive mood has been frequently remarked on, and I think that it has to be explained on the ground that truth to her is often *provisional*; to one constitutionally timid, and scrupulously truthful, the subjunctive mood would come naturally. We may say that the use of the indicative implies confidence, the use of the subjunctive uncertainty.

> They say that time assuages.
> Time never did assuage.
> An actual suffering strengthens
> As sinews do, with age.
>
> Time is a test of trouble
> But not a remedy.

If such it prove, it prove too
There was no malady.

There is here a characteristic shift from the mood of confident
assertion in the first stanza to that of uncertainty in the second;
we may say, of course, that the second 'prove' in the penultimate
line is just careless. The American critic Yvor Winters[1] speaks
of Emily's 'habitual carelessness'. But since this sort of shift
is so common, we should do well to consider whether it is not
deliberate. Surely there may here be an elliptical suggestion of
'will prove' or 'may prove'. The statement that the alleged
healing power of time is an illusion is thus made less absolute.
She is not committed to the judgement that a person who has
been cured of a sorrow never really felt sorrow. Naturally the
assertion would be stronger without the subjunctive, but it
would be less honest. Emily wishes to explore moral truth, not
to preach. There are also in plenty, especially during the period
of Emily's greatest creative power, poems of confident assertion,
strongly indicative in mood, like *Because I could not stop for
death* (No. 103).

As for the irregularity of Emily's rhymes and rhythms, it is
difficult to find any consistent explanation, or any principle in
which they can be said to occur deliberately. Emily composed
by instinct—which is not to say automatically. She used the
basic rhythms of the hymns she had heard from childhood, ·
adapting them to the need of the moment. Her instinct told her
that mechanical regularity makes for monotony. Her rhythms,
considered as personal variations on a rigid pattern, are to be
justified, or found wanting, according to the shapes and sounds

[1] *Maule's Curse*. New Directions, 1938. Like Blackmur Winters combines
perfunctory praise ('she is one of the greatest lyric poets of all time') with a
general attitude of severe disapproval. After quoting *I like to see it lap the miles*
(No. 85), he says: 'The poem is abominable; and the quality of silly playfulness
which renders it abominable is diffused more or less perceptibly throughout
most of her work . . .' I have given earlier my reasons for insisting that these
weaker poems must be ignored—though I do not agree with what Winters says
of *I like to see it lap the miles*.

of particular poems. To my ear her rhythmic sense is seldom absolutely deficient, often inspired. There is more variety than the formal appearance of the poems would suggest, and a study of the rhythmic variations in any half-dozen of her best poems would reveal considerable subtlety.

Attempts have been made to show that her use of assonance instead of full rhyme is always deliberate artistry. It would be truer to say that, on the whole though not invariably, full rhyme accompanies her moods of confidence, and assonance her moods of uncertainty. But the exceptions are significant. All we can say is that she felt no particular compulsion to find exact rhymes, and that probably assonance also helped her to get away from the mechanical jingle of hymn-forms.

Some may be satisfied to condemn what they call her 'carelessness', or to say that she had no technique, or to regard her stylistic irregularities as a proof of eccentricity or amateurishness. I prefer to say that there are many possible causes for poetic failure, and that technical inadequacy is not the most important. A feeble poem is not redeemed by exact rhymes, correct grammar and rhythmical regularity. Not all the technical elegance of, say, Austin Dobson's *vers de société* can bring it to life: on the contrary, the craftsmanship only serves to emphasise the essential emptiness. Emily was concerned with the realization of a vision or a truth in language—the right word took priority over technical conformity. When she was wholly inspired, technique, as it were, rose to the occasion; when she was not, technique failed as well as language. Emily had no excess of technical ease with which to disguise a central failure of inspiration. It would be idle to deny that there are technical blemishes which Emily herself, had she had the benefit of sound advice and the desire to perfect her poems for public inspection, would have wished to correct. But we must take her poems for what they are: if any are good, they are technically good. There is no such thing as a good poem which is technically bad. We have to do with a poet of almost total originality, and it is very rarely that originality and formal perfection go together. There is about all original poets— Skelton, Donne, Blake, Hardy, Hopkins—a certain home-made roughness of form which, according to temperament, some will regard as a blessing, and some as a blemish. Ben Jonson regarded Donne's metrical irregularity as a blemish, and on the whole posterity has disagreed with Jonson.

It is when we come to look at Emily's ideas, and the language in which she expresses them, that we are most struck by her originality and her audacity. To read, for instance, *A bird came down the walk* (No. 52) is to feel that we have never seen a bird before—or rather, that we have never noticed the birds we constantly see.

> He glanced with rapid eyes
> That hurried all around;
> They looked like frightened beads, I thought.

Here, the faithful realization of the state of perpetual insecurity in which a bird lives owes everything to a primitive act of self-identification with the bird. It is as if Emily's own timidity were dissolved in the bird's. It is subjectivity carried to the point of self-annihilation. We are reminded of Keats' sparrow picking about among the gravel. I cannot follow a critic who calls Emily sophisticated. She had, at such moments as these, a purely primitive vision; there is nothing of the *faux naïf* in her descriptive writing.

There is in this poem a certain cool brilliance, a certain hard objectivity of outward appearance which is often revealed when the poet is in fact most engaged. She lived her poems, and never simply thought them; they were paid for in sensibility or in suffering or in ecstasy. She had many costly failures, but no cheap successes. In *The last night that she lived* (No. 140) it is evident that the poet is acutely involved, and for that reason she is careful to overstate nothing: the poem begins almost casually. In comparison with most conventional elegies its tone is off-hand. Then, with the utmost economy of language, the changing emotions of the watchers are described as the moment of death approaches. When the moment comes, the watchers are temporarily ignored: four lines are given to the supreme instant—

> She mentioned, and forgot;
> Then lightly as a reed
> Bent to the water, struggled scarce,
> Consented, and was dead.

The simile in the second and third lines is chosen with a skill or insight which cannot be analysed—we recall that to Emily water was usually a symbol of eternity. Then in the final stanza the unspoken feelings of the onlookers are again expressed. I doubt if a deathbed has ever been more indelibly realized in words. Emily's own phrase 'a nearness to tremendousness' comes to mind; always when she is nearest to tremendousness she speaks most quietly. At the deathbed the feeling of awe is uppermost: the sense of loss will come later, but for the present all purely human feeling is numbed. One has to go back to *The Lyke-Wake Dirge* to find anything so deliberately impressive in its holding back of the forces of dissolution and annihilation. After reading such a poem as this, one does not speak of technique.

When she appears most cool, most off-hand, most nearly approaching flippancy, we should be especially on our guard against missing her profoundest significances. It is difficult to say exactly what experience is recorded in the extraordinary and tantalizing poem *I started early, took my dog* (No. 76). It is evident that here the sea represents some overwhelming force, of great destructive power—death possibly, or love, or perhaps both. To ships on the sea the poet appears to be a mouse—symbol of timidity. What begins in a playful vein concludes as a pursuit to the death. It is only when she reaches the solid

1

familiarity of home, the reassurance of the town she knows so well, that the pursuit ends.

Such a poem as this holds a kind of compulsion not to be explained by anything we can be sure it means. Far more comprehensible, but no less mysterious, is *Because I could not stop for death* (No. 103). This is one of the best of those poems in which Emily triumphs over death by accepting it, calmly, civilly, as befits a gentlewoman receiving the attentions of a gentleman. It is an essay in death-in-life. Only by civilizing death and by familiarizing herself with it can it be brought within the scheme of what is tolerable and credible. The tone is tenderly ironic, the atmosphere tinged with sorrow for life and concern for the smallness of the human soul that must face inexorable death, solitary except for its immortality. The poem is simple, almost commonplace, yet the mystery that pervades it is inexhaustible. There is, within this mystery, a sense of reconciliation. To find anything like it we have to go to Prospero's closing speeches in *The Tempest*.

In order to apprehend, if not to understand, the sources of Emily Dickinson's mystery, we have to consider her language. It would be a long and rewarding study to examine Emily's use of words in constructing the world in which she lived out her poems. There is no room here for such a study, but the following passage from Allen Tate's essay would form a valuable starting-point.

> The two elements of her style, considered as a point of view, are immortality, or the idea of permanence, and the physical process of death or decay. Her diction has two corresponding features: words of Latin or Greek origin and, sharply opposed to these, the concrete Saxon element. It is this verbal conflict that gives to her verse its high tension; it is not a device deliberately seized upon, but a feeling for language that senses out the two fundamental components of English and their metaphysical relation: the Latin for ideas and the Saxon for perceptions—the peculiar virtue of English as a poetic language.

This applies to all poets writing in English who have a true insight into the nature of their medium. Yet not all poets, endowed as they were with this uniquely poetic medium, have recognized its peculiar quality. Shakespeare undoubtedly did:

> If thou didst ever hold me in thy heart,
> Absent thee from felicity awhile,
> And in this harsh world draw thy breath in pain,
> To tell my story.

The dignity of abstract ideas is here combined and contrasted with the pathos of simple human suffering to achieve that balance of intellect and senses which is fundamental to the apprehension of life in poetic terms. It is in lines like these that we find, if anywhere, the *meaning* of life. Possibly Emily learned the secret from Shakespeare, whom she read constantly. At all events this Shakespearean accent, the balance between the abstract quality of Romance words and the concrete actuality of the Saxon, is never far from her poetry at its finest.

J. R.

Chalfont St Giles,
1958

lii

SELECTED POEMS

I

Whether my bark went down at sea,
Whether she met with gales,
Whether to isles enchanted
She bent her docile sails,

By what mystic mooring
She is held today—
This is the errand of the eye
Out upon the bay.

2

Success is counted sweetest
By those who ne'er succeed.
To comprehend a nectar
Requires sorest need.

Not one of all the purple host
Who took the flag today
Can tell the definition
So clear of victory

As he defeated, dying,
On whose forbidden ear
The distant strains of triumph
Burst agonized and clear.

3

Exultation is the going
Of an inland soul to sea,
Past the houses, past the headlands,
Into deep eternity.

Bred as we, among the mountains,
Can the sailor understand
The divine intoxication
Of the first league out from land?

4

I never hear the word 'escape'
Without a quicker blood,
A sudden expectation,
A flying attitude.

I never hear of prisons broad
By soldiers battered down
But I tug childish at my bars
Only to fail again.

5

Our lives are Swiss,
So still, so cool,
Till some odd afternoon
The Alps neglect their curtains
And we look farther on.

Italy stands the other side
While, like a guard between,
The solemn Alps,
The siren Alps,
Forever intervene.

6

Heart, not so heavy as mine
Wending late home,
As it passed my window
Whistled itself a tune—
A careless snatch, a ballad,
A ditty of the street,
Yet to my irritated ear
An anodyne so sweet,
It was as if a bobolink
Sauntering this way
Carolled, and paused, and carolled,
Then bubbled slow away.
It was as if a chirping brook
Upon a dusty way
Set bleeding feet to minuets
Without the knowing why.
Tomorrow, night will come again,
Perhaps weary and sore.
Ah bugle! by my window
I pray you pass once more.

7

My nosegays are for captives—
Dim, long expectant eyes,
Fingers denied the plucking,
Patient till Paradise.

To such, if they should whisper
Of morning and the moor,
They bear no other errand,
And I no other prayer.

8

One dignity delays for all,
One mitred afternoon,
None can avoid this purple,
None evade this crown.

Coach it insures and footmen,
Chamber, and state, and throng,
Bells also in the village
As we ride grand along.

What dignified attendants,
What service when we pause,
How loyally at parting
Their hundred hats they raise!

How pomp surpassing ermine
When simple You and I
Present our meek escutcheon
And claim the rank to die!

4

9

New feet within my garden go—
New fingers stir the sod.
A troubadour upon the elm
Betrays the solitude.

New children play upon the green—
New weary sleep below,
And still the pensive spring returns,
And still the punctual snow.

10

To hang our head ostensibly,
And subsequent, to find
That such was not the posture
Of our immortal mind

Affords the sly presumption
That in so dense a fuzz
You too take cobweb attitudes
Upon a plane of gauze.

11

Surgeons must be very careful
When they take the knife.
Underneath their fine incisions
Stirs the culprit, life.

12

What inn is this
Where for the night
Peculiar traveller comes?
Who is the landlord?
Where the maids?
Behold, what curious rooms!
No ruddy fires on the hearth—
No brimming tankards flow.
Necromancer! Landlord!
Who are these below?

13

A something in a summer's day
As slow her flambeaux burn away
Which solemnizes me.

A something in a summer's noon—
A depth, an azure, a perfume—
Transcending ecstasy.

And still within a summer's night
A something so transporting bright
I clap my hands to see,

Then veil my too inspecting face
Lest such a subtle, shimmering grace
Flutter too far for me.

The wizard fingers never rest,
The purple brook within the breast
Still chafes its narrow bed.

Still rears the east her amber flag,
Guides still the sun along the crag
His caravan of red.

So looking on the night, the morn
Conclude the wonder gay—
And I meet, coming through the dews
Another summer's day.

14

In lands I never saw, they say
Immortal Alps look down
Whose bonnets touch the firmament,
Whose sandals touch the town,

Meek at whose everlasting feet
A myriad daisy play.
Which, sir, are you and which am I
Upon an August day?

15

For each ecstatic instant
We must an anguish pay
In keen and quivering ratio
To the ecstasy.

7

For each beloved hour
Sharp pittances of years,
Bitter contested farthings,
And coffers heaped with tears.

16

Bring me the sunset in a cup,
Reckon the morning's flagons up
And say how many dew,
Tell me how far the morning leaps,
Tell me what time the weaver sleeps
Who spun the breadths of blue.

Write me how many notes there be
In the new robin's extasy
Among astonished boughs,
How many trips the tortoise makes,
How many cups the bee partakes,
The debauchee of dews.

Also, who laid the rainbow's piers,
Also, who leads the docile spheres
By withes of supple blue?
Whose fingers string the stalactite,
Who counts the wampum of the night
To see that none is due?

Who built this little alban house
And shut the windows down so close
My spirit cannot see?
Who'll let me out some gala day
With implements to fly away,
Passing pomposity?

17

Water is taught by thirst,
Land by the oceans passed,
Transport by throe,
Peace by its battles told,
Love by memorial mold,
Birds by the snow.

18

An altered look about the hills,
A Tyrian light the village fills,
A wider sunrise in the morn,
A deeper twilight on the lawn,
A print of a vermillion foot,
A purple finger on the slope,
A flippant fly upon the pane,
A spider at his trade again,
An added strut in Chanticleer,
A flower expected everywhere,
An axe shrill singing in the woods,
Fern odors on untravelled roads—
All this and more I cannot tell.
A furtive look you know as well.
And Nicodemus' mystery
Receives its annual reply.

19

Just lost when I was saved,
Just felt the world go by,
Just girt me for the onset with eternity,
When breath blew back,
And on the other side
I heard recede the disappointed tide.

Therefore as one returned I feel,
Odd secrets of the line to tell—
Some sailor skirting foreign shores,
Some pale reporter from the awful doors
Before the seal.

Next time, to stay.
Next time, the things to see
By ear unheard,
Unscrutinized by eye—

Next time, to tarry,
While the ages steal,
Slow tramp the centuries,
And the cycles wheel.

A wounded deer leaps highest,
I've heard the hunter tell.
'Tis but the ecstasy of death,
And then the brake is still.

The smitten rock that gushes,
The trampled steel that springs!
A cheek is always redder
Just where the hectic stings.

Mirth is the mail of anguish,
In which it cautious arm
Lest anybody spy the blood
And 'You're hurt' exclaim.

21

To learn the transport by the pain
As blind men learn the sun,
To die of thirst suspecting
That brooks in meadows run,

To stay the homesick, homesick feet
Upon a foreign shore,
Haunted by native lands the while,
And blue, beloved air—

This is the sovereign anguish,
This the signal woe.
These are the patient laureates
Whose voices, trained below,

Ascend in ceaseless carol,
Inaudible indeed
To us, the duller scholars
Of the mysterious bard.

'Tis so much joy! 'tis so much joy!
If I should fail, what poverty!
And yet, as poor as I
Have ventured all upon a throw,
Have gained—yes, hesitated so,
This side the victory.

Life is but life, and death but death.
Bliss is but bliss, and breath but breath.
And if indeed I fail,
At least to know the worst is sweet.
Defeat means nothing but defeat,
No drearier can befall.

And if I gain—Oh gun at sea,
Oh bells that in the steeples be,
At first repeat it slow!
For Heaven is a different thing,
Conjectured and waked sudden in,
And might extinguish me.

23

Faith is a fine invention
When gentlemen can see,
But microscopes are prudent
In an emergency.

24

I shall know why, when time is over,
And I have ceased to wonder why;
Christ will explain each separate anguish
In the fair schoolroom of the sky.

He will tell me what Peter promised,
And I, for wonder at his woe,
I shall forget the drop of anguish
That scalds me now, that scalds me now.

25

On this long storm the rainbow rose,
On this late morn the sun,
The clouds like listless elephants
Horizons straggled down.

The birds rose smiling in their nests
The gales indeed were done.
Alas, how heedless were the eyes
On whom the summer shone!

The quiet nonchalance of death
No daybreak can bestir.
The slow archangel's syllables
Must awaken her.

26

Two swimmers wrestled on the spar
Until the morning sun.
When one turned smiling to the land,
Oh God, the other one!

The stray ships, passing,
Spied a face
Upon the waters borne
With eyes in death still begging raised
And hands beseeching thrown.

27

I should not dare to leave my friend,
Because—because if he should die
While I was gone, and I too late
Should reach the heart that wanted me,

If I should disappoint the eyes
That hunted—hunted so to see,
And could not bear to shut until
They noticed me—they noticed me,

If I should stab the patient faith
So sure I'd come—so sure I'd come,
It listening—listening went to sleep
Telling my tardy name,

My heart would wish it broke before,
Since breaking then—since breaking then
Were useless as next morning's sun
Where midnight frosts had lain.

28

I taste a liquor never brewed
From tankards scooped in pearl.
Not all the Frankfort berries
Yield such an alcohol.

Inebriate of air am I
And debauchee of dew,
Reeling through endless summer days
From inns of molten blue.

When landlords turn the drunken bee
Out of the foxglove's door,
When butterflies renounce their drams,
I shall but drink the more,

Till seraphs swing their snowy hats
And saints to windows run
To see the little tippler
From Manzanilla come!

29

Safe in their alabaster chambers,
Untouched by morning
And untouched by noon,
Sleep the meek members of the resurrection—
Rafter of satin,
And roof of stone.

Light laughs the breeze
In her castle above them,
Babbles the bee in a stolid ear,
Pipe the sweet birds in ignorant cadence—
Ah, what sagacity perished here!

Alternative versions of second stanza. (See note p. 103.)

Grand go the years in the crescent above them,
Worlds scoop their arcs
And firmaments row,
Diadems drop and Doges surrender,
Soundless as dots on a disc of snow.

Springs shake the sills
But the echoes stiffen,
Hoar is the window
And numb the door.
Tribes of eclipse in tents of marble
Staples of ages have buckled there.

Springs shake the seals
But the silence stiffens,
Frosts unhook in the Northern zones,
Icicles crawl from Polar caverns,
Midnight in marble refutes the suns.

30

God permits industrious angels
Afternoons to play.
I met one, forgot my schoolmates
All for him straightway.

God calls home the angers promply
At the setting sun.
I missed mine. How dreary, marbles
After playing crown!

31

The sun just touched the morning.
The morning, happy thing,
Supposed that he had come to dwell
And life would all be spring.

She felt herself supremer,
A raised, ethereal thing.
Henceforth for her what holiday!
Meanwhile her wheeling king
Trailed slow along the orchards
His haughty spangled hems,
Leaving a new necessity,
The want of diadems.

The morning fluttered, staggered,
Felt feebly for her crown,
Her unanointed forehead
Henceforth her only one.

32

Heaven is what I cannot reach.
The apple on the tree,
Provided it do hopeless hang,
That Heaven is to me.

The colour on the cruising cloud,
The interdicted land
Behind the hill, the house behind,
There paradise is found.

Her teazing purples, afternoons,
The credulous decoy,
Enamored of the conjuror
That spurned us yesterday.

33

I like a look of agony
Because I know it's true.
Men do not sham convulsion
Nor simulate a throe.

The eyes glaze once, and that is death—
Impossible to feign
The beads upon the forehead
By homely anguish strung.

34

Wild nights—wild nights!
Were I with thee,
Wild nights should be
Our luxury.

Futile the winds
To a heart in port
Done with the compass,
Done with the chart.

Rowing in Eden—
Ah, the sea!
Might I but moor tonight
In thee.

35

Hope is the thing with feathers
That perches in the soul
And sings the tune without the words
And never stops at all,

And sweetest in the gale is heard;
And sore must be the storm
That could abash the little bird
That kept so many warm.

I've heard it in the chillest land
And on the strangest sea,
Yet never in extremity
It asked a crumb of me.

36

There's a certain slant of light,
Winter afternoons,
That oppresses like the heft
Of cathedral tunes.

Heavenly hurt it gives us.
We can find no scar
But internal difference
Where the meanings are.

None may teach it any—
'Tis the seal despair,
An imperial affliction
Sent us of the air.

When it comes the landscape listens,
Shadows hold their breath.
When it goes 'tis like the distance
On the look of death.

37

Good night! Which put the candle out?
A jealous zephyr, not a doubt.
Ah, friend, you little knew
How long at that celestial wick
The angels laboured diligent,
Extinguished now for you.

It might have been the lighthouse spark
Some sailor rowing in the dark
Had importuned to see.
It might have been the waning lamp
That lit the drummer from the camp
To purer reveille.

38

Read, sweet, how others strove,
Till we are stouter;
What they renounced,
Till we are less afraid;
How many times they bore the faithful witness,
Till we are helped
As if a kingdom cared.

Read then of faith
That shone above the fagot,
Clear strains of hymn
The river could not drown,
Brave names of men
And celestial women
Passed out of record
Into renown.

39

A solemn thing it was, I said,
A woman white to be,
And wear, if God should count me fit,
Her blameless mystery;

A timid thing, to drop a life
Into the mystic well,
Too plummetless that it come back
Eternity until.

I pondered how the bliss would look,
And would it feel as big
When I could take it in my hand
As hovering seen through fog.

And then the size of this 'small' life—
The sages call it small—
Swelled like horizons in my breast
And I sneered softly—'Small'!

40

I felt a funeral in my brain,
And mourners to and fro
Kept treading, treading, till it seemed
That sense was breaking through.

And when they all were seated,
A service like a drum
Kept beating, beating, till I thought
My mind was going numb.

And then I heard them lift a box
And creak across my soul
With those same boots of lead again,
Then space began to toll,

As all the Heavens were a bell,
And being but an ear,
And I and silence some strange race
Wrecked solitary here.

And then a plank in reason broke,
And I dropped down and down
And hit a world at every plunge,
And finished knowing then.

41

A clock stopped—
Not the mantel's.
Geneva's farthest skill
Can't put the puppet bowing
That just now dangled still.

An awe came on the trinket.
The figures hunched with pain
Then quivered out of decimals
Into degreeless noon.

It will not stir for doctors,
This pendulum of snow.
The shopman importunes it,
While cool concernless No

Nods from the gilded pointers,
Nods from the seconds slim,
Decades of arrogance between
The dial life
And him.

42

I'm nobody. Who are you?
Are you nobody too?
Then there's a pair of us.
Don't tell—they'd banish us, you know.

How dreary to be somebody,
How public—like a frog—
To tell your name the livelong June
To an admiring bog.

43

I know some lonely houses off the road
A robber'd like the look of—
Wooden barred,
And windows hanging low,
Inviting to
A portico,
Where two could creep;
One hand the tools,
The other peep
To make sure all's asleep—
Old fashioned eyes
Not easy to surprise!

How orderly the kitchen'd look by night,
With just a clock,
But they could gag the tick,
And mice won't bark;
And so the walls don't tell,
None will.

A pair of spectacles ajar just stir;
An almanac's aware.
Was it the mat winked,
Or a nervous star?
The moon slides down the stair
To see who's there.

There's plunder, where
Tankard or spoon,
Earring or stone,
A watch, some ancient brooch
To match the grandmama
Staid sleeping there.

Day rattles too;
Stealth's slow.
The sun has got as far
As the third sycamore.
Screams Chanticleer
'Who's there?'

And echoes, trains away,
Sneer 'Where?'
While the old couple, just astir,
Fancy the sunrise left the door ajar.

44

The soul selects her own society,
Then shuts the door.
To her divine majority
Present no more.

Unmoved she notes the chariots pausing
At her low gate;
Unmoved, an Emperor be kneeling
Upon her mat.

I've known her from an ample nation
Choose one,
Then close the valves of her attention
Like stone.

45

The day came slow till five o'clock
Then sprang before the hills
Like hindered rubies or the light
A sudden musket spills.

The purple could not keep the east
The sunrise shook abroad
Like breadths of topaz, packed a-night,
The lady just unrolled.

The happy winds their timbrels took;
The birds in docile rows
Arranged themselves around their prince :
The wind is prince of those.

The orchard sparkled like a Jew.
How mighty 'twas to be
A guest in this stupendous place,
The parlor of the day.

46

It sifts from leaden sieves,
It powders all the wood.
If fills with alabaster wool
The wrinkles of the road.

It makes an even face
Of mountain and of plain,
Unbroken forehead from the east
Unto the east again.

It reaches to the fence,
It wraps it rail by rail
Till it is lost in fleeces;
It deals celestial veil.

To stump and stack and stem,
A summer's empty room,
Acres of joints where harvests were,
Recordless but for them.

It ruffles wrists of posts
As ankles of a queen,
Then stills its artisans like ghosts,
Denying they have been.

47

I should have been too glad, I see,
Too lifted for the scant degree
Of life's penurious round;
My little circuit would have shamed
This new circumference, have blamed
The homelier time behind.

I should have been too saved, I see,
Too rescued; fear too dim to me
That I could spell the prayer
I knew so perfect yesterday,
That scalding one, 'Sabachthani',
Recited fluent here.

Earth would have been too much, I see,
And Heaven not enough for me.
I should have had the joy
Without the fear to justify,
The palm without the Calvary.
So, Savior, crucify.

Defeat whets victory, they say.
The reefs in old Gethsemane
Endear the shore beyond.
'Tis beggars banquets best define,
'Tis thirsting vitalizes wine.
Faith bleats to understand.

48

He fumbles at your soul
As players at the keys
Before they drop full music on.
He stuns you by degrees,
Prepares your brittle nature
For the ethereal blow
By fainter hammers further heard,
Then nearer, then so slow
Your breath has time to straighten,
Your brain to bubble cool,
Deals one imperial thunderbolt
That scalps your naked soul.

When winds take forests in their paws
The universe is still.

There came a day at summer's full
Entirely for me;
I thought that such were for the saints,
Where resurrections be.

The sun as common went abroad,
The flowers accustomed blew,
As if no soul the solstice passed
That maketh all things new.

The time was scarce profaned by speech;
The symbol of a word
Was needless, as at sacrament
The wardrobe of our lord.

Each was to each the sealed church,
Permitted to commune this time,
Lest we too awkward show
At supper of the lamb.

The hours slid fast as hours will,
Clutched tight by greedy hands;
So faces on two decks look back,
Bound to opposing lands.

And so when all the time had leaked,
Without external sound
Each bound the other's crucifix,
We gave no other bond—

Sufficient troth that we shall rise,
Deposed at length the grave,
To that new marriage,
Justified through Calvaries of love.

As if I asked a common alms,
And in my wondering hand
A stranger pressed a kingdom,
And I, bewildered, stand—
As if I asked the orient
Had it for me a morn,
And it should lift its purple dykes,
And shatter me with dawn!

Before I got my eye put out
I liked as well to see
As others creatures that have eyes
And know no other way;

But were it told to me today
That I might have the sky
For mine, I tell you that my heart
Would split for size of me—

The meadows mine,
The mountains mine,
All forests, stintless stars,
As much of noon as I could take
Between my finite eyes,

The motions of the dipping birds,
The morning's amber road
For mine to look at when I liked,
The news would strike me dead;

So safer guess, with just my soul
Upon the window pane,
Where other creatures put their eyes
Incautious of the sun.

52

A bird came down the walk.
He did not know I saw.
He bit an angleworm in halves
And ate the fellow raw,

And then he drank a dew
From a convenient grass,
And then hopped sidewise to the wall
To let a beetle pass.

He glanced with rapid eyes
That hurried all around;
They looked like frightened beads, I thought;
He stirred his velvet head

Like one in danger, cautious;
I offered him a crumb,
And he unrolled his feathers
And rode him softer home

31

Than oars divide the ocean,
Too silver for a seam,
Or butterflies off banks of noon
Leap, plashless as they swim.

53

When night is almost done
And sunrise grows so near
That we can touch the spaces,
It's time to smooth the hair

And get the dimples ready,
And wonder we could care
For that old, faded midnight
That frightened but an hour.

54

I dreaded that first robin so,
But he is mastered now;
I'm some accustomed to him grown—
He hurts a little, though.

I thought if I could only live
Till that first shout got by,
Not all pianos in the woods
Had power to mangle me.

I dared not meet the daffodils
For fear their yellow gown
Would pierce me with a fashion
So foreign to my own.

I wished the grass would hurry,
So when 'twas time to see,
He'd be too tall, the tallest one
Could stretch to look at me.

I could not bear the bees should come;
I wished they'd stay away
In those dim countries where they go.
What word had they for me?

They're here though; not a creature failed.
No blossom stayed away
In gentle deference to me,
The Queen of Calvary,

Each one salutes me as he goes,
And I my childish plumes
Lift, in bereaved acknowledgement
Of their unthinking drums.

55

I gained it so—
By climbing slow,
By catching at the twigs that grow
Between the bliss and me.
It hung so high,
As well the sky
Attempt by strategy

I said I gained it—
This was all.
Look, how I clutch it
Lest it fall,
And I a pauper go
Unfitted by an instant's grace
For the contented beggar's face
I wore an hour ago.

56

It struck me every day.
The lightning was as new
As if the cloud that instant slit
And let the fire through.

It burned me in the night,
It blistered to my dream,
It sickened fresh upon my sight
With every morn that came.

I thought that storm was brief—
The maddest, quickest by,
But nature lost the date of this
And left it in the sky.

57

A precious, mouldering pleasure 'tis
To meet an antique book
In just the dress his century wore;
A privilege, I think,

34

His venerable hand to take,
And warming in our own,
A passage back or two to make
To times when he was young,

His quaint opinions to inspect,
His thought to ascertain
On themes concern our mutual mind—
The literature of man,

What interested scholars most,
What competitions ran
When Plato was a certainty
And Sophocles a man,

When Sappho was a living girl,
And Beatrice wore
The gown that Dante deified.
Facts centuries before

He traverses, familiar
As one should come to town
And tell you all your dreams were true.
He lived where dreams were born,

His presence is enchantment.
You beg him not to go;
Old volumes shake their vellum heads
And tantalize just so.

58

No rack can torture me,
My soul at liberty;
Behind this mortal bone
There knits a bolder one

You cannot prick with saw
Nor pierce with scimitar.
Two bodies therefore be.
Bind one, the other fly.

The eagle of his nest
No easier divest
And gain the sky
Than mayest thou,

Except thyself may be
Thine enemy;
Captivity is consciousness,
So's liberty.

59

There's been a death in the opposite house
As lately as today.
I know it by the numb look
Such houses have alway.

The neighbours rustle in and out;
The doctor drives away.
A window opens like a pod,
Abrupt, mechanically;

Somebody flings a mattress out.
The children hurry by;
They wonder if it died on that.
I used to, when a boy.

The minister goes stiffly in
As if the house were his
And he owned all the mourners now,
And little boys besides;

And then the milliner, and the man
Of the appalling trade
To take the measure of the house.
There'll be that dark parade

Of tassels and of coaches soon.
It's easy as a sign—
The intuition of the news
In just a country town.

60

What soft cherubic creatures
These gentlewomen are.
One would as soon assault a plush
Or violate a star.

Such dimity convictions,
A horror so refined
Of freckled human nature,
Of deity ashamed—

It's such a common glory,
A fisherman's degree.
Redemption, brittle lady,
Be so ashamed of thee.

61

It might be lonelier
Without the loneliness.
I'm so accustomed to my fate,
Perhaps the other peace

Would interrupt the dark
And crowd the little room
Too scant by cubits to contain
The sacrament of him.

I am not used to hope.
It might intrude upon
Its sweet parade, blaspheme the place
Ordained to suffering.

It might be easier
To fail with land in sight
Than gain my blue peninsula
To perish of delight.

62

I read my sentence steadily,
Reviewed it with my eyes
To see that I made no mistake
In its extremest clause—
The date and manner of the shame
And then the pious form
That 'God have mercy' on the soul
The jury voted him.

I made my soul familiar with her extremity,
That at the last it should not be a novel agony,
But she and death acquainted
Meet tranquilly, as friends
Salute and pass without a hint,
And there the matter ends.

63

Not in this world to see his face
Sounds long, until I read the place
Where this is said to be
But just the primer to a life
Unopened, rare, upon the shelf
Clasped yet to him and me;

And yet my primer suits me so,
I would not choose a book to know
Than that be sweeter wise.
Might someone else so learned be
And leave me just my A B C,
Himself could have the skies.

64

Much madness is divinest sense
To a discerning eye—
Much sense the starkest madness.
'Tis the majority
In this, as all, prevail.
Assent and you are sane;
Demur, you're straightway dangerous
And handled with a chain.

65

The wind tapped like a tired man
And like a host 'Come in'
I boldly answered. Entered then
My residence within

A rapid footless guest,
To offer whom a chair
Were as impossible as hand
A sofa to the air.

No bone had he to bind him;
His speech was like the push
Of numerous humming birds at once
From a superior bush;

His countenance a billow;
His fingers as he passed
Let go a music as of tunes
Blown tremulous in glass.

He visited still flitting,
Then like a timid man
Again he tapped. 'Twas flurriedly,
And I became alone.

66

This is my letter to the world
That never wrote to me,
The simple news that nature told
With tender majesty.

Her message is committed
To hands I cannot see.
For love of her, sweet countrymen,
Judge tenderly of me.

67

I died for beauty, but was scarce
Adjusted in the tomb
When one who died for truth was lain
In an adjoining room.

He questioned softly why I failed,
'For beauty' I replied.
'And I for truth. Themself are one.
We bretheren are' he said.

And so, as kinsmen met a night,
We talked between the rooms,
Until the moss had reached our lips
And covered up our names.

68

I heard a fly buzz when I died.
The stillness in the room
Was like the stillness in the air
Between the heaves of storm.

The eyes around had wrung them dry,
And breaths were gathering firm
For that last onset when the king
Be witnessed in the room.

I willed my keepsakes, signed away
What portion of me be
Assignable; and then it was
There interposed a fly

With blue uncertain stumbling buzz
Between the light and me;
And then the windows failed; and then
I could not see to see.

69

Civilization spurns the leopard.
Was the leopard bold?
Deserts never rebuked her satin,
Ethiop her gold.
Tawny her customs,
She was conscious;
Spotted her dun gown.
This was the leopard's nature, Signor—
Need a keeper frown?

Pity the pard that left her Asia.
Memories of palm
Cannot be stifled with narcotic
Nor suppressed with balm.

70

Going to him—happy letter!
Tell him,
Tell him the page I didn't write.
Tell him I only said the syntax
And left the verb and the pronoun out.

Tell him just how the fingers hurried,
Then how they waded slow, slow;
And then you wished you had eyes in your pages
So you could see what moved them so.

Tell him it wasn't a practised writer—
You guessed from the way the sentence toiled.
You could hear the bodice tug behind you
As if it held but the might of a child.
You almost pitied it, you it worked so.
Tell him—no, you may quibble there,
For it would split his heart to know it,
And then you and I were silenter.

Tell him night finished before we finished,
And the old clock kept neighing 'Day!'
And you got sleepy and begged to be ended.
What could hinder it, so to say?
Tell him just how she sealed you, cautious.
But if he ask where you are hid
Until tomorrow, happy letter,
Gesture coquette, and shake your head.

71

As far from pity as complaint,
As cool to speech as stone,
As numb to revelation
As if my trade were bone,

As far from time as history,
As near yourself today
As children to the rainbow's scarf,
Or sunset's yellow play

To eyelids in the sepulchre,
How dumb the dancer lies
While color's revelations break
And blaze the butterflies!

72

I envy seas whereon he rides,
I envy spokes of wheels
Of chariots that him convey,
I envy crooked hills

That gaze upon his journey.
How easy all can see
What is forbidden utterly,
As Heaven, unto me!

I envy nests of sparrows
That dot his distant eaves,
The wealthy fly upon his pane.
The happy, happy leaves

That just abroad his window
Have summer's leave to play,
The ear rings of Pizarro
Could not obtain for me.

I envy light that wakes him
And bells that boldly ring
To tell him it is noon abroad;
Myself be noon to him.

Yet interdict my blossom
And abrogate my bee,
Lest noon in everlasting night
Drop Gabriel and me.

73

He touched me, so I live to know
That such a day, permitted so,
I groped upon his breast;
It was a boundless place to me
And silenced as the awful sea
Puts minor streams to rest.

And now I'm different from before
As if I breathed superior air
Or brushed a royal gown—
My feet too that had wandered so,
My gypsy face transfigured now
To tenderer renown.

Into this port if I might come,
Rebecca to Jerusalem
Would not so ravished turn,
Nor Persian, baffled at her shrine,
Lift such a crucifixal sign
To her imperial sun.

If anybody's friend be dead,
It's sharpest of the theme
The thinking how they walked alive
At such and such a time;

Their costume of a Sunday,
Some manner of the hair,
A prank nobody knew but them,
Lost in the sepulchre;

How warm they were on such a day—
You almost feel the date,
So short way off it seems—
And now they're centuries from that;

How pleased they were at what you said—
You try to touch the smile
And dip your fingers in the frost;
When was it—can you tell?—

You asked the company to tea;
Acquaintance, just a few,
And chatted close with this grand thing
That don't remember you,

Past bows and invitations,
Past interview and vow,
Past what ourself can estimate—
That makes the quick of woe.

It was not death, for I stood up,
And all the dead lie down.
It was not night, for all the bells
Put out their tongues for noon.

It was not frost, for on my flesh
I felt siroccos crawl;
Nor fire, for just my marble feet
Could keep a chancel cool—

And yet it tasted like them all.
The figures I have seen
Set orderly for burial
Reminded me of mine,

As if my life were shaven
And fitted to a frame
And could not breathe without a key;
And 'twas like midnight some

When everything that ticked has stopped
And space stares all around,
Or grisly frosts, first Autumn morns,
Repeal the beating ground,

But most like chaos—stopless, cool,
Without a chance or spar,
Or even a report of land
To justify despair.

I started early, took my dog,
And visited the sea.
The mermaids in the basement
Came out to look at me

And frigates in the upper floor
Extended hempen hands,
Presuming me to be a mouse
Aground upon the sands,

But no man moved me till the tide
Went past my simple shoe
And past my apron and my belt
And past my bodice too,

And made as he would eat me up
As wholly as a dew
Upon a dandelion's sleeve;
And then I started too

And he, he followed close behind;
I felt his silver heel
Upon my ankle, then my shoes
Would overflow with pearl,

Until we met the solid town.
No one he seemed to know
And bowing with a mighty look
At me, the sea withdrew.

77

Mine by the right of the white election—
Mine by the royal seal—
Mine by the sign in the scarlet prison
Bars cannot conceal!

Mine here in vision and in veto—
Mine by the grave's repeal,
Title confirmed
Delirious charter—
Mine long as ages steal!

78

The heart asks pleasure first,
And then excuse from pain,
And then those little anodynes
That deaden suffering,

And then to go to sleep,
And then if it should be
The will of its inquisitor
The privilege to die.

79

I took my power in my hand
And went against the world;
'Twas not so much as David had
But I was twice as bold.

I aimed my pebble, but myself
Was all the one that fell—
Was it Goliah was too large
Or was myself too small?

80

I've seen a dying eye
Run round and round a room
In search of something as it seemed,
Then cloudier become,
And then obscure with fog,
And then be soldered down
Without disclosing what it be
'Twere blessed to have seen.

81

I measure every grief I meet
With narrow, probing eyes;
I wonder if it weighs like mine
Or has an easier size.

I wonder if they bore it long,
Or did it just begin;
I could not tell the date of mine,
It feels so old a pain.

I wonder if it hurts to live
And if they have to try,
And whether, could they choose between,
It would not be to die.

I note that some, gone patient long,
At length renew their smile,
An imitation of a light
That has so little oil.

I wonder if, when years have piled
Some thousands on the harm
That hurt them early, such a lapse
Could give them any balm.

Or would they go on aching still
Through centuries of nerve,
Enlightened to a larger pain
In contrast with the love.

The grieved are many, I am told.
There is the various cause.
Death is but one and comes but once
And only nails the eyes

There's grief of want, and grief of cold,
A sort they call despair;
There's banishment from native eyes
In sight of native air,

And though I may not guess the kind
Correctly, yet to me
A piercing comfort it affords,
In passing Calvary,

To note the fashions of the Cross
And how they're mostly worn,
Still fascinated to presume
That some are like my own.

82

I had been hungry all the years.
My noon had come to dine.
I trembling drew the table near
And touched the curious wine.

'Twas this on tables I had seen
When turning hungry home
I looked in windows for the wealth
I could not hope for mine.

I did not know the ample bread.
'Twas so unlike the crumb
The birds and I had often shared
In nature's dining room.

The plenty hurt me, 'twas so new.
Myself felt ill and odd,
As berry of a mountain bush
Transplanted to the road.

Nor was I hungry, so I found
That hunger was a way
Of persons outside windows
The entering takes away.

83

I gave myself to him,
And took himself for pay.
The solemn contract of a life
Was ratified this way.

The wealth might disappoint,
Myself a poorer prove
Than this great purchaser suspect,
The daily own of love

Depreciate the vision;
But till the merchant buy,
Still fable in the Isles of Spice
The subtle cargoes lie.

At least 'tis mutual risk,
Some found it mutual gain,
Sweet debt of life each night to owe,
Insolvent every noon.

84

I found the words to every thought
I ever had but one,
And that defies me
As a hand did try to chalk the sun
The races nurtured in the dark.
How would your own begin?
Can blaze be shown in cochineal
Or noon in mazarin?

85

I like to see it lap the miles
And lick the valleys up,
And stop to feed itself at tanks
And then prodigious step

Around a pile of mountains,
And supercilious peer
In shanties by the sides of roads,
And then a quarry pare

To fit its sides
And crawl between
Complaining all the while
In horrid, hooting stanza,
Then chase itself down hill

And neigh like Boanerges,
Then prompter than a star,
Stop, docile and omnipotent,
At its own stable door.

86

I years had been from home
And now before the door
I dared not enter, lest a face
I never saw before

Stare stolid into mine
And ask my business there—
My business but a life I left :
Was such remaining there?

I leaned upon the awe
I lingered with before.
The second life an ocean rolled
And broke against my ear.

I laughed a crumbling laugh
That I could fear a door
Who consternation compassed
And never winced before.

I fitted to the latch
My hand with trembling care,
Lest back the awful door should spring
And leave me in the floor;

Then moved my fingers off
As cautiously as glass,
And held my ears, and like a thief
Fled gasping from the house.

87

Our journey had advanced,
Our feet were almost come
To that odd fork in being's road,
Eternity by term.

Our pace took sudden awe,
Our feet reluctant led;
Before were cities, but between,
The forest of the dead.

Retreat was out of hope;
Behind, a sealed route,
Eternity's white flag before,
And God at every gate.

55

It makes no difference abroad.
The seasons fit the same.
The mornings blossom into noons
And split their pods of flame.

Wild flowers kindle in the woods.
The brooks slam all the day.
No black bird bates his banjo
For passing Calvary.

Auto da fe and judgment
Are nothing to the bee;
His separation from his rose
To him sums misery.

The way I read a letter's this :
'Tis first I lock the door
And push it with my fingers next
For transport it be sure;

And then I go the furthest off
To counteract a knock,
Then draw my little letter forth
And slowly pick the lock;

Then glancing narrow at the wall
And narrow at the floor
For firm conviction of a mouse
Not exorcised before,

Peruse how infinite I am
To no one that you know,
And sigh for lack of heaven, but not
The heaven God bestow.

90

I cannot live with you.
It would be life,
And life is over there
Behind the shelf

The sexton keeps the key to,
Putting up
Our life, his porcelain,
Like a cup

Discarded of the housewife,
Quaint or broke;
A newer Sevres pleases,
Old ones crack.

I could not die with you;
For one must wait
To shut the other's gaze down.
You could not,

And I—could I stand by
And see you freeze
Without my right of frost,
Death's privilege?

Nor could I rise with you,
Because your face
Would put Jesus';
That new grace

Grow plain and foreign
On my homesick eye,
Except that you than he
Shone closer by.

They'd judge us—how?
For you served heaven, you know,
Or sought to;
I could not,

Because you saturated sight
And I had no more eyes
For sordid excellence,
As Paradise;

And were you lost, I would be,
Though my name
Rang loudest
On the heavenly fame;

And were you saved
And I condemned to be
Where you were not,
That self were hell to me.

So we must meet apart,
You there, I here
With just the door ajar
That oceans are, and prayer,
And that white sustenance,
Despair.

Pain has an element of blank.
It cannot recollect
When it begun or if there were
A time when it was not.

It has no future but itself;
Its infinite contain
Its past, enlightened to perceive
New periods of pain.

A prison gets to be a friend,
Between its ponderous face
And ours a kinsmanship express;
And in its narrow eyes

We come to look with gratitude
For the appointed beam
It deal us, stated as our food
And hungered for the same.

We learn to know the planks
That answer to our feet,
So miserable a sound at first,
Nor even now so sweet

As plashing in the pools
When memory was a boy
But a demurer circuit,
A geometric joy.

The posture of the key
That interrupt the day
To our endeavor—not so real
The cheek of liberty

As this phantasm steel,
Whose features day and night
Are present to us as our own
And as escapeless quite.

The narrow round, the stint,
The slow exchange of hope
For something passiver—content
Too steep for looking up,

The liberty we knew
Avoided like a dream
Too wide for any night but Heaven,
If that indeed redeem.

93

A long, long sleep, a famous sleep
That makes no show for morn
By stretch of limb or stir of lid,
An independent one—

Was ever idleness like this,
Upon a bank of stone
To bask the centuries away
Nor once look up for noon?

94

The name of it is Autumn,
The hue of it is blood,
An artery upon the hill,
A vein along the road,

Great globules in the alleys,
And oh, the shower of stain
When winds upset the basin
And spill the scarlet rain.

It sprinkles bonnets far below,
It gathers ruddy pools,
Then eddies like a rose away
Upon vermillion wheels.

95

Of all the souls that stand create
I have elected one.
When sense from spirit files away
And subterfuge is done,
When that which is and that which was
Apart, intrinsic stand,
And this brief tragedy of flesh
Is shifted like a sand,
When figures show their royal front
And mists are carved away,
Behold the atom I preferred
To all the lists of clay.

One need not be a chamber to be haunted,
One need not be a house.
The brain has corridors surpassing
Material place.

Far safer, of a midnight meeting
External ghost,
Than its interior confronting
That cooler host.

Far safer, through an abbey gallop,
The stones a-chase,
Than unarmed one's a-self encounter
In lonesome place.

Ourself behind ourself concealed
Should startle most;
Assassin hid in our apartment
Be horror's least.

The body borrows a revolver;
He bolts the door,
O'erlooking a superior spectre
Or more.

Essential oils are wrung.
The attar from the rose
Be not expressed by suns alone—
It is the gift of screws.

The general rose decay,
But this in lady's drawer
Make summer when the lady lie
In ceaseless rosemary.

98

The soul unto itself
Is an imperial friend,
Or the most agonizing spy
An enemy could send.

Secure against its own,
No treason it can fear.
Itself its sovreign, of itself
The soul should stand in awe.

99

They say that time assuages.
Time never did assuage.
An actual suffering strengthens
As sinews do, with age.

Time is a test of trouble
But not a remedy.
If such it prove, it prove too
There was no malady.

100

Victory comes late
And is held low to freezing lips
Too rapt with frost
To take it.
How sweet it would have tasted—
Just a drop.
Was God so economical?
His table's spread too high for us
Unless we dine on tiptoe.
Crumbs fit such little mouths;
Cherries suit robins;
The eagle's golden breakfast strangles them.
God keeps his oath to sparrows
Who of little love know how to starve.

101

The sun kept setting, setting still.
No hue of afternoon
Upon the village I perceived.
From house to house 'twas noon.

The dusk kept dropping, dropping still.
No dew upon the grass
But only on my forehead stopped
And wandered in my face.

My feet kept drowsing, drowsing still.
My fingers were awake.
Yet why so little sound myself
Unto my seeming make?

How well I knew the light before.
I could not see it now.
'Tis dying I am doing, but
I'm not afraid to know.

102

Their hight in Heaven comforts not
Their glory nought to me.
'Twas best imperfect, as it was;
I'm finite—I can't see

The house of supposition;
The glimmering frontier
That skirts the acres of perhaps
To me shows insecure.

The wealth I had contented me
If 'twas a meaner size,
Then I had counted it until
It pleased my narrow eyes

Better than larger values
That show however true.
This timid life of evidence
Keeps pleading 'I don't know'.

103

Because I could not stop for Death
He kindly stopped for me.
The carriage held but just ourselves
And immortality.

We slowly drove. He knew no haste,
And I had put away
My labour and my leisure too
For his civility.

We passed the school where children strove
At recess in the ring.
We passed the fields of gazing grain;
We passed the setting sun—

Or rather, he passed us.
The dews drew quivering and chill,
For only gossamer my gown,
My tippet only tulle.

We paused before a house that seemed
A swelling of the ground.
The roof was scarcely visible,
The cornice in the ground.

Since then 'tis centuries, and yet
Feels shorter than the day
I first surmised the horses' heads
Were toward Eternity.

104

We thirst at first—'tis nature's act—
And later, when we die,
A little water supplicate
Of fingers going by.

It intimates the finer want
Whose adequate supply
Is that great water in the west
Termed Immortality.

105

Alter! When the hills do.
Falter! When the sun
Question if his glory
Be the perfect one.

Surfeit! When the daffodil
Doth of the dew.
Even as herself, sir,
I will of you.

106

She rose to his requirement—dropped
The playthings of her life
To take the honorable work
Of woman and of wife.

If aught she missed in her new day
Of amplitude or awe,
Or first prospective, or the gold
In using wear away,

It lay unmentioned as the sea
Develop pearl and weed,
But only to himself be known
The fathoms they abide.

107

I many times thought peace had come
When peace was far away,
As wrecked men deem they sight the land
At centre of the sea

And struggle slacker but to prove
As hopelessly as I
How many the fictitious shores
Or any harbor be.

108

Remorse is memory awake,
Her parties all astir,
A presence of departed acts
At window and at door.

It's past set down before the soul
And lighted with a match,
Perusal to facilitate
And help belief to stretch.

Remorse is cureless—the disease
Not even God can heal,
For 'tis his institution and
The adequate of Hell.

109

It dropped so low in my regard
I heard it hit the ground
And go to pieces on the stones
At bottom of my mind;

Yet blamed the fate that fractured less
Than I reviled myself
For entertaining plated wares
Upon my silver shelf.

110

My life had stood, a loaded gun,
In corners till a day
The owner passed, identified,
And carried me away;

And now we roam in sovreign woods,
And now we hunt the doe,
And every time I speak for him
The mountains straight reply.

And do I smile, such cordial light
Upon the valley glow
It is as a Vesuvian face
Had let its pleasure through;

And when at night, our good day done,
I guard my master's head,
'Tis better than the eider duck's
Deep pillow to have shared.

To foe of his I'm deadly foe;
None stir the second time
On whom I lay a yellow eye
Or an emphatic thumb.

Though I than he may longer live,
He longer must than I,
For I have but the power to kill
Without the power to die.

III

One blessing had I than the rest
So larger to my eyes
That I stopped gauging, satisfied
For this enchanted size.

It was the limit of my dream,
The focus of my prayer,
A perfect, paralyzing bliss,
Contented as despair.

I knew no more of want or cold,
Phantasms both become,
For this new value in the soul,
Supremest earthly sum,

The heaven below the Heaven above
Obscured with ruddier blue,
Life's latitudes leant over, full;
The judgment perished too.

Why bliss so scantily disburse,
Why paradise defer,
Why floods be served to us in bowls
I speculate no more.

112

Presentiment is that long shadow on the lawn
Indicative that suns go down,
The notice to the startled grass
That darkness is about to pass

113

The wind begun to knead the grass
As women do a dough;
He flung a handful at the plain,
A handful at the sky.
The leaves unhooked themselves from trees
And started all abroad;
The dust did scoop itself like hands
And throw away the road.

The wagons quickened on the street;
The thunders gossiped low;
The lightning showed a yellow head
And then a livid toe.
The birds put up the bars to nests;
The cattle flung to barns.
Then came one drop of giant rain;
And then, as if the hands
That held the dams had parted hold,
The waters wrecked the sky,
But overlooked my father's house,
Just quartering a tree.

114

The only news I know
Is bulletins all day
From immortality;

The only shows I see
Tomorrow and today,
Perchance eternity.

The only one I meet
Is God, the only street
Existence; this traversed,

If other news there be
Or admirabler show,
I'll tell it you

115

The robin is the one
That interrupt the morn
With hurried, few, express reports
When March is scarcely on.

The robin is the one
That overflow the noon
With her cherubic quantity,
An April but begun.

The robin is the one
That speechless from her nest
Submit that home and certainty
And sanctity are best.

116

Ample make this bed;
Make this bed with awe.
In it wait till judgment break
Excellent and fair.

Be its mattress straight;
Be its pillow round;
Let no sunrise' yellow noise
Interrupt this ground.

117

Finite to fail, but infinite to venture.
For the one ship that struts the shore
Many's the gallant, overwhelmed creature
Nodding in navies nevermore.

118

I sing to use the waiting,
My bonnet but to tie
And shut the door unto my house.
No more to do have I

Till, his best step approaching,
We journey to the day
And tell each other how we sung
To keep the dark away.

119

Split the lark and you'll find the music,
Bulb after bulb in silver rolled,
Scantily dealt to the summer morning,
Saved for your ear when lutes be old.

Loose the flood; you shall find it patent,
Gush after gush reserved for you.
Scarlet experiment! Sceptic Thomas,
Now do you doubt that your bird was true?

120

I stepped from plank to plank,
A slow and cautious way;
The stars about my head I felt,
About my feet the sea.

I knew not but the next
Would be my final inch.
This gave me that precarious gait
Some call experience.

121

We outgrow love like other things
And put it in a drawer,
Till it an antique fashion shows
Like costumes grandsires wore.

122

To my quick ear the leaves conferred;
The bushes they were bells.
I could not find a privacy
From nature's sentinels.

In cave if I presumed to hide,
The walls begun to tell.
Creation seemed a mighty crack
To make me visible.

123

It is an honorable thought
And makes one lift one's hat,
As one met sudden gentlefolk
Upon a daily street,

That we've immortal place
Though pyramids decay
And kingdoms like the orchard
Flit russetly away.

124

A door just opened on a street;
I, lost, was passing by;
An instant's width of warmth disclosed,
And wealth, and company.

The door as instant shut; and I,
I lost, was passing by—
Lost doubly, but by contrast most,
Informing misery.

The mountain sat upon the plain
In his tremendous chair,
His observation omnifold,
His inquest everywhere.

The seasons played around his knees
Like children round a sire;
Grandfather of the days is he,
Of dawn the ancestor.

This merit hath the worst:
It cannot be again.
When fate hath taunted last
And thrown her furthest stone,

The maimed may pause and breathe
And glance securely round.
The deer attracts no further
Than it resists the hound.

A narrow fellow in the grass
Occasionally rides.
You may have met him—did you not?
His notice sudden is.

The grass divides as with a comb,
A spotted shaft is seen,
And then it closes at your feet
And opens further on.

He likes a boggy acre,
A floor too cool for corn;
Yet when a boy and barefoot,
I more than once at noon

Have passed, I thought, a whiplash
Unbraiding in the sun;
When, stooping to secure it,
It wrinkled and was gone.

Several of nature's people
I know, and they know me;
I feel for them a transport
Of cordiality,

But never met this fellow,
Attended or alone,
Without a tighter breathing
And zero at the bone.

128

The leaves like women interchange
Sagacious confidence—
Somewhat of nods, and somewhat
Portentous inference,

The parties in both cases
Enjoining secrecy,
Inviolable compact
To notoriety.

129

This was in the white of the year;
That was in the green.
Drifts were as difficult then to think
As daisies now to be seen.

Looking back is best that is left,
Or if it be before,
Retrospection is prospect's half,
Sometimes almost more.

130

Superfluous were the sun
When excellence be dead.
He were superfluous every day,
For every day be said

That syllable whose faith
Just saves it from despair,
And whose 'I'll meet you' hesitates
If love inquire 'Where?'

Upon his dateless fame
Our periods may lie,
As stars that drop anonymous
From an abundant sky.

131

The stimulus beyond the grave
His countenance to see
Supports me like imperial drams
Afforded day by day.

132

How still the bells in steeples stand
Till swollen with the sky,
They leap upon their silver feet
In frantic melody.

133

The dying need but little, dear—
A glass of water's all,
A flower's unobtrusive face
To punctuate the wall,

A fan perhaps, a friend's regret,
And certainty that one
No colour in the rainbow
Perceive when you are gone.

134

I never saw a moor;
I never saw the sea.
Yet know I how the heather looks
And what a billow be.

I never spoke with God,
Nor visited in Heaven.
Yet certain am I of the spot
As if the checks were given.

135

I had a daily bliss
I half indifferent viewed,
Till sudden I perceived it stir;
It grew as I pursued,

Till when around a hight
It wasted from my sight,
Increased beyond my utmost scope
I learned to estimate.

Title divine is mine—
The wife without the sign,
Acute degree conferred on me:
Empress of Calvary—
Royal all but the crown,
Betrothed without the swoon
God sends us women
When you hold garnet to garnet,
Gold to gold.
Born, bridalled, shrouded
In a day.
'My husband' women say,
Stroking the melody.
Is *this* the way?

The sky is low, the clouds are mean.
A travelling flake of snow
Across a barn or through a rut
Debates if it will go.

A narrow wind complains all day
How someone treated him.
Nature, like us, is sometimes caught
Without her diadem.

138

At half past three a single bird
Unto a silent sky
Propounded but a single term
Of cautious melody.

At half past four experiment
Had subjugated test,
And lo, her silver principle
Supplanted all the rest.

At half past seven element
Nor implement be seen,
And place was where the presence was,
Circumference between.

139

My cocoon tightens; colors tease;
I'm feeling for the air.
A dim capacity for wings
Demeans the dress I wear.

A power of butterfly must be.
The aptitude to fly
Meadows of majesty concedes
And easy sweeps of sky.

So I must baffle at the hint
And cipher at the sign,
And make much blunder if at last
I take the clue divine.

The last night that she lived,
It was a common night
Except the dying—this to us
Made nature different.

We noticed smallest things,
Things overlooked before,
By this great light upon our minds
Italicised, as 'twere.

As we went out and in
Between her final room
And rooms where those to be alive
Tomorrow were, a blame

That others could exist
While she must finish quite,
A jealousy for her arose
So nearly infinite.

We waited while she passed;
It was a narrow time.
Too jostled were our souls to speak.
At length the notice came.

She mentioned, and forgot;
Then lightly as a reed
Bent to the water, struggled scarce,
Consented, and was dead.

And we, we placed the hair
And drew the head erect;
And then an awful leisure was,
Belief to regulate.

141

The crickets sang,
And set the sun,
And workmen finished one by one
Their seam the day upon.

The low grass loaded with the dew;
The twilight stood as strangers do
With hat in hand, polite and new,
To stay as if, or go.

A vastness as a neighbour came,
A wisdom without face or name,
A peace as hemispheres at home—
And so the night became.

142

After a hundred years
Nobody knows the place,
Agony that enacted there
Motionless as peace.

Weeds triumphant ranged.
Strangers strolled and spelled
At the lone orthography
Of the elder dead.

Winds of summer fields
Recollect the way,
Instinct picking up the key
Dropped by memory.

143

Great streets of silence led away
To neighborhoods of pause.
Here was no notice, no dissent,
No universe, no laws.

By clocks 'twas morning, and for night
The bells at distance called,
But epoch had no basis here
For period exhaled.

144

The clouds their backs together laid,
The north begun to push,
The forests galloped till they fell,
The lightning played like mice,

The thunder crumbled like a stuff.
How good to be in tombs
Where nature's temper cannot reach
Nor missile ever comes.

145

When I hoped, I feared;
Since I hoped, I dared;
Everywhere alone
As a church remain.
Spectre cannot harm;
Serpent cannot charm.
He deposes doom
Who hath suffered him.

146

Remembrance has a rear and front.
'Tis something like a house.
It has a garret also
For refuse and the mouse,

Besides the deepest cellar
That ever mason laid.
Look to it, by its fathoms
Ourselves be not pursued.

147

Too few the mornings be,
Too scant the nights.
No lodging can be had
For the delights
That come to earth to stay
But no apartment find
And ride away.

148

Immortal is an ample word
When what we need is by,
But when it leaves us for a time
'Tis a necessity.

Of Heaven above the firmest proof
We fundamental know,
Except for its marauding hand
It had been Heaven below.

149

The show is not the show
But they that go.
Menagerie to me
My neighbor be.
Fair play
Both went to see.

150

He preached upon 'Breadth' till it argued him narrow—
The broad are too broad to define;
And of 'Truth', until it proclaimed him a liar,
The truth never flaunted a sign.

Simplicity fled from his counterfeit presence
As gold the pyrites would shun.
What confusion would cover the innocent Jesus
To meet so enabled a man!

151

We like March.
His shoes are purple;
He is new and high.
Makes he mud for dog and peddler;
Makes he forests dry.
Knows the adder tongue his coming
And presents her spot.
Stands the sun so close and mighty
That our minds are hot.

News is he of all the others.
Bold it were to die
With the blue birds exercising
On his British sky.

152

A deed knocks first at thought,
And then it knocks at will.
That is the manufactoring spot.
And, will at home and well,

It then goes out an act,
Or is entombed so still
That only to the ear of God
Its doom is audible.

153

Like trains of cars on tracks of plush
I hear the level bee.
A jar across the flowers goes;
Their velvet masonry

Withstands until the sweet assault
Their chivalry consumes,
While he victorious tilts away
To vanquish other blooms.

154

A word dropped careless on a page
May stimulate an eye
When folded in perpetual seam
The wrinkled maker lie.

Infection in the sentence breeds.
We may inhale despair
At distances of centuries
From the malaria.

155

There is no frigate like a book
To take us lands away,
Nor any coursers like a page
Of prancing poetry.
This travel may the poorest take
Without offence of toll.
How frugal is the chariot
That bears the human soul.

156

Is Heaven a physician?
They say that he can heal,
But medicine posthumous
Is unavailable.
Is Heaven an exchequer?
They speak of what we owe,
But that negotiation
I'm not a party to.

157

The spider as an artist
Has never been employed,
Though his surpassing merit
Is freely certified

By every broom and Bridget
Throughout a Christian land—
Neglected son of genius,
I take thee by the hand.

158

While we were fearing it, it came,
But came with less of fear
Because that fearing it so long
Had almost made it fair.

There is a fitting—a dismay;
A fitting—a despair.
'Tis harder knowing it is due
Than knowing it is here.

The trying on the utmost,
The morning it is new,
Is terribler than wearing it
A whole existence through.

159

Let me not mar that perfect dream
By an auroral stain,
But so adjust my daily night
That it will come again.

Not when we know, the power accosts;
The garment of surprise
Was all our timid mother wore
At home in Paradise.

160

Trusty as the stars
Who quit their shining working,
Prompt as when I lit them
In Genesis' new house,
Durable as dawn
Whose antiquated blossom
Makes a world's suspense
Perish and rejoice.

161

What mystery pervades a well!
The water lives so far—
A neighbor from another world
Residing in a jar

Whose limit none have ever seen,
But just his lid of glass,
Like looking every time you please
In an abyss's face.

The grass does not appear afraid.
I often wonder he
Can stand so close and look so bold
At what is awe to me.

Related somehow they may be;
The sedge stands next the sea
Where he is floorless
And does no timidity betray.

But nature is a stranger yet;
The ones that cite her most
Have never passed her haunted house
Nor simplified her ghost.

To pity those that know her not
Is helped by the regret
That those who know her know her less
The nearer her they get.

162

Belshazzar had a letter,
He never had but one.
Belshazzar's correspondent
Concluded and begun
In that immortal copy;
The conscience of us all
Can read without its glasses
On revelation's wall.

163

'Tis whiter than an Indian pipe;
'Tis dimmer than a lace;
No stature has it, like a fog
When you approach the place.
Not any voice imply it here
Or intimate it there.
A spirit—how doth it accost,
What function hath the air?
This limitless hyperbole
Each one of us shall be.
'Tis drama if (hypothesis)
It be not tragedy.

164

We shall find the cube of the rainbow—
Of that there is no doubt;
But the arc of a lover's conjecture
Eludes the finding out.

165

The dandelion's pallid tube
Astonishes the grass,
And winter instantly becomes
An infinite Alas.
The tube uplifts a signal bud
And then a shouting flower,
The proclamation of the suns
That sepulture is o'er.

166

Hope is a subtle glutton,
He feeds upon the fair;
And yet, inspected closely,
What abstinence is there.

His is the halcyon table
That never seats but one,
And whatsoever is consumed
The same amount remain.

167

The bat is dun, with wrinkled wings,
Like fallow article;
And not a song pervade his lips,
Or none perceptible;

His small umbrella quaintly halved
Describing in the air
An arc alike inscrutable—
Elate philosopher,

Deputed from what firmament,
Of what astute abode,
Empowered with what malignity
Auspiciously withheld.

To his adroit creator
Ascribe no less the praise—
Beneficent, believe me,
His eccentricities.

The farthest thunder that I heard
Was nearer than the sky,
And rumbles still, though torrid noons
Have lain their missiles by.
The lightning that preceded it
Struck no one but myself,
But I would not exchange the bolt
For all the rest of life.
Indebtedness to oxygen
The happy may repay,
But not the obligation
To electricity.
It founds the homes and decks the days,
And every clamor bright
Is but the gleam concomitant
Of that waylaying light.
The thought is quiet as a flake,
A crash without a sound,
How life's reverberation
Its explanation found.

There came a wind like a bugle.
It quivered through the grass,
And a green chill upon the heat
So ominous did pass.
We barred the windows and the doors
As from an emerald ghost.

The doom's electric moccasin
That very instant passed.
On a strange mob of panting trees
And fences fled away
And rivers where the houses ran
Those looked that lived that day.
The bell within the steeple wild
The flying tidings told—
How much can come
And much can go,
And yet abide the world.

170

Few, yet enough—
Enough is one.
To that ethereal throng
Have not each one of us the right
To stealthily belong?

171

Of God we ask one favor,
That we may be forgiven—
For what, he is presumed to know:
The crime from us is hidden.
Immured the whole of life
Within a magic prison,
We reprimand the happiness
That too competes with Heaven.

172

To try to speak, and miss the way,
And ask it of the tears
Is gratitude's sweet poverty,
The tatters that he wears.

A better coat if he possess
Would help him to conceal,
Not subjugate, the mutineer
Whose title is the soul.

173

Circumference, thou bride of awe,
Possessing, thou shalt be
Possessed by every hallowed knight
That dares to covet thee.

174

A sloop of amber slips away
Upon an ether sea,
And wrecks in peace a purple tar,
The son of ecstasy.

175

A face devoid of love or grace,
A hateful, hard, successful face,
A face with which a stone
Would feel as thoroughly at ease
As were they old acquaintances
First time together thrown.

176

My life closed twice before its close.
It yet remains to see
If immortality unveil
A third event to me,

So huge, so hopeless to conceive
As these that twice befel.
Parting is all we know of heaven,
And all we need of hell.

177

Sweet is the swamp with its secrets,
Until we meet a snake;
'Tis then we sigh for houses
And our departure take
At that enthralling gallop
That only childhood knows.
A snake is summer's treason
And guile is where it goes.

178

The distance that the dead have gone
Does not at first appear;
Their coming back seems possible
For many an ardent year.

And then that we have followed them
We more than half suspect,
So intimate have we become
With their dear retrospect.

179

The reticent volcano keeps
His never slumbering plan;
Confided are his projects pink
To no precarious man.

If nature will not tell the tale
Jehovah told to her,
Can human nature not survive
Without a listener?

Admonished by her buckled lips
Let every babbler be;
The only secret people keep
Is immortality.

180

Where every bird is bold to go
And bees abashless play,
The foreigner before he knocks
Must thrust the tears away.

181

The saddest noise, the sweetest noise,
The maddest noise that grows,
The birds, they make it in the spring,
At night's delicious close

Between the March and April line,
That magical frontier
Beyond which summer hesitates,
Almost too heavenly near.

It makes us think of all the dead
That sauntered with us here,
By separation's sorcery
Made cruelly more dear.

It makes us think of what we had,
And what we now deplore.
We almost wish those siren throats
Would go, and sing no more.

An ear can break a human heart
As quickly as a spear;
We wish the ear had not a heart
So dangerously near.

NOTE ON THE CHRONOLOGY

I HAVE adopted the chronological arrangement of Thomas H. Johnson's edition, and I would here add Mr. Johnson's own word of warning: 'The dating of them is conjectural and for the most part will always remain so.'

The following is a table of dates, giving the numbers of the poems in the present selection, and the conjectural year of composition.

1	1858	145–147	1871
2–18	1859	148–153	1872
19–28	1860	154–158	1873
29–43	1861	159	1875
44–98 *and* 136 (out of sequence in Harvard edition) 1862		160	1876
		161	not known
99–111	1863	162–163	1879
112–126	1864	164	1880
127–135	1865	165	1881
137–140	1866	166–168	1882
141	1867	169	1883
142	1869	170–177	1884
143–144	1870	178–181	not known

NOTES

6. **HEART, NOT SO HEAVY AS MINE**
Title supplied by ED in a letter: *Whistling under my Window*.

16. **BRING ME THE SUNSET IN A CUP**
alban: White—that is, the body, by which the spirit is imprisoned.

17. **WATER IS TAUGHT BY THIRST**
mold: picture or photograph.

18. **AN ALTERED LOOK ABOUT THE HILLS**
Nicodemus' mystery: Nicodemus questioned Jesus about re-birth (John iii. 4).

28. **I TASTE A LIQUOR NEVER BREWED**
Frankfort berries: grapes used in making German wine.
Manzanilla: name of a brand of sherry, but not a place-name, as ED seems to think. Johnson assumes that she means Manzanillo, a port in Cuba.
When this poem was published anonymously in the *Springfield Daily Republican*, May 4, 1861, under the title *The May-Wine*, the text was editorially emended, lines 3–4 appearing as
> Not Frankfort berries yield the sense
> Such a delicious whirl.

29. **SAFE IN THEIR ALABASTER CHAMBERS**
The two stanzas of this poem were published anonymously, with one minor change, in the *Springfield Daily Republican* on March 1, 1862 under the title *The Sleeping*. The three alternative second stanzas were written in response to criticisms of the original second stanza ('Light laughs the breeze') by ED's sister-in-law, Susan Gilbert, whose opinion that the first stanza is complete and admits of no worthy sequel deserves our respect—superb as are all the four second stanzas.
In a note written to ED about this poem Sue says: 'It just occurs to me that the first verse is complete in itself. If needs no other and can't be coupled. . . . You never made a peer for that verse and I *guess* your

kingdom doesn't hold one—I always go to the fire and get warm after thinking of it, but I never *can* again. . . .'

There is a striking parallel between Sue's last sentence and something ED wrote in a letter to Higginson about 1870: 'If I read a book and it makes my whole body so cold no fire can ever warm me, I know that is poetry. If I feel physically as if the top of my head were taken off, I know that is poetry. These are the only ways I know it. Is there any other way?' The egregious Higginson called this a 'crowning extravaganza' when writing of ED's 'eccentricities' after her death.

It is probable that ED had discussed these physical symptoms with Sue much earlier. They have a significant resemblance to those described by A. E. Housman in his lecture on *The Name and Nature of Poetry*.

36. THERE'S A CERTAIN SLANT OF LIGHT
heft: weight.

43. I KNOW SOME LONELY HOUSES OFF THE ROAD
And so the walls don't tell: i.e. so long as.

45. THE DAY CAME SLOW TILL FIVE O'CLOCK
Stanza 2 exemplifies the awkwardness sometimes arising from ED's habit of omitting the relative pronoun: 'which' is to be understood immediately before 'The sunrise' and also before 'The lady'.

46. IT SIFTS FROM LEADEN SIEVES
The title *Snow* was given by ED in a letter.

47. I SHOULED HAVE BEEN TOO GLAD, I SEE
Sabachthani: the words of Jesus on the Cross, meaning 'Why hast thou forsaken me?'
to justify: i.e. which would have justified the joy.

50. AS IF I ASKED A COMMON ALMS
Included in a letter to T. W. Higginson of June, 1862. She is expressing her sense of obligation for his help as a preceptor.

54. I DREADED THAT FIRST ROBIN SO
some: somewhat—a common American usage.
The Queen of Calvary: ED regarded herself as uncrowned 'queen' to the Rev. Charles Wadsworth of Philadelphia, whose appointment to the Calvary Church, San Francisco, was announced in January 1862. The crushing effect of the news is the inspiration of this poem.

59. THERE'S BEEN A DEATH IN THE OPPOSITE HOUSE

When a boy: to have referred to herself in childhood as a girl would no doubt have seemed to ED an over-particularisation. If 'man' means 'mankind', 'boy' means 'the child'. See also *A narrow fellow in the grass,* No. 127.

63. NOT IN THIS WORLD TO SEE HIS FACE

I would not choose . . .: I would not choose to know any book which might be more sweetly wise than that (i.e. my primer).

72. I ENVY SEAS WHEREON HE RIDES

Pizarro: the Pizarro brothers, early sixteenth century explorers, were associated with the conquest of the wealthy Spanish empire in Peru.

73. HE TOUCHED ME, SO I LIVE TO KNOW

Persian: the Jewish woman Esther, wife of Ahasuerus (Xerxes), king of Persia in the fifth century B.C.

75. IT WAS NOT DEATH, FOR I STOOD UP

some: see note on No. 54.

77. MINE BY THE RIGHT OF THE WHITE ELECTION

This is one of that series of intensely personal, almost private, poems written about 1862 to express her love for Charles Wadsworth from whom she was now, as it seemed, permanently separated. Paradoxically, the fact that she could never have married him, and was now permanently separated, so long as she could achieve the final act of renunciation, could be felt as a triumph.

The white election: refers not only to her practice, begun about this time, of dressing in white, but also to her acceptance of perpetual chastity.

royal seal: may be connected with her assumption of the title of 'Queen of Calvary' (see No. 54).

the grave's repeal: she believed that death would repeal the veto which separated them in life.

85. I LIKE TO SEE IT LAP THE MILES

Boanerges: Sons of thunder (see Mark iii 17).

The railway to Amherst had been opened only recently.

87. OUR JOURNEY HAD ADVANCED

that odd fork: cf. a letter to ED's cousins in 1861. 'Your letters are all real, just the tangled road children walked before you, some of them to the end, and others but a little way, even as far as the fork in the road.'

ED wrote another version of this poem, as follows. I give the text with her own punctuation and stanza divisions.

> The Wind begun to rock the Grass
> With threatening Tunes and low—
> He threw a Menace at the Earth—
> A Menace at the Sky.
>
> The Leaves unhooked themselves from Trees—
> And started all abroad
> The Dust did scoop itself like Hands
> And threw away the Road.
>
> The Wagons quickened on the Streets
> The Thunder hurried slow—
> The Lightning showed a Yellow Beak
> And then a livid Claw.
>
> The Birds put up the Bars to Nests—
> The Cattle fled to Barns—
> There came one drop of Giant Rain
> And then as if the Hands
>
> That held the Dams had parted hold
> The Waters Wrecked the Sky,
> But overlooked my Father's House—
> Just quartering a Tree—

119. SPLIT THE LARK AND YOU'LL FIND THE MUSIC

It is clear that ED is thinking of herself as the lark, whose songs, like her poems, have been 'scantily dealt' out during life, but will be found inside her by any doubting Thomas sceptical of the truth of her love. The word *bulb* in line 2 is difficult to explain by reference to its botanical meaning; the suggestion is perhaps rather of a series of swellings in a glass tube.

For *Sceptic Thomas* see John xx 24–25. See also ED's letter to Theodore Holland, 1885: 'Thomas's faith in anatomy was stronger than his faith in faith'.

123. IT IS AN HONORABLE THOUGHT

russetly: evidently an original coinage.

124. **A DOOR JUST OPENED ON A STREET**
Informing misery: the contrast between the sociable scene behind the
door and her own loneliness, by thus 'informing' her of her misery,
made her feel even more lost than before.

125. **THE MOUNTAIN SAT UPON THE PLAIN**
omnifold: an original coinage.

127. **A NARROW FELLOW IN THE GRASS**
when a boy: see note on No. 59.

128. **THE LEAVES LIKE WOMEN INTERCHANGE**
Cf. No. 122.

134. **I NEVER SAW A MOOR**
As if the checks were given: as if the railway tickets were already
surrendered (to the conductor). Compare the American colloquialism
'to hand in one's checks'—that is, to die.

136. **TITLE DIVINE IS MINE.**
Empress of Calvary: see note on No. 54.

140. **THE LAST NIGHT THAT SHE LIVED**
The occasion of this may have been the death in May 1866 of Laura
Dickey, daughter of a lifelong neighbour of the Dickinson family in
Amherst.

150. **HE PREACHED UPON 'BREADTH' TILL IT ARGUED HIM NARROW**
pyrites: metallic ore resembling gold but of low value.
enabled: the MSS. provide a number of alternatives, e.g. *religious,
accomplished, discerning, accoutred, established, conclusive.*

151. **WE LIKE MARCH**
exercising: a MS. variant is 'buccaneering'.

162. **BELSHAZZAR HAD A LETTER**
See Daniel V. I am not certain that I have punctuated this correctly:
the only punctuation in the MS. copies consists of three dashes—after
lines 1, 2, and 8 respectively.

163. **'TIS WHITER THAN AN INDIAN PIPE**
First published in 1896 under the title *The Spirit.*
Indian pipe: small plant of a white, waxy appearance which grows
in damp woods in North America, especially on decaying vegetation.
Sometimes called 'corpse-plant' or 'ghost-flower'.

174. A SLOOP OF AMBER SLIPS AWAY

Written, apparently, two years before her death, these four lines exemplify the compression and symbolic richness of ED's style at its best. She was always fascinated by sunset, which to her mind was closely connected with the idea of immortality. I think *tar* must be taken as meaning 'sailor', since it is referred to as *the son of ecstasy*. The *sloop of amber* is the dying sun which, in departing, blots out a purple cloud (likened to a shipwrecked sailor). *Ecstasy* refers to the full brightness of the evening sun, which was the cause of the purple colour of the cloud.

176. MY LIFE CLOSED TWICE BEFORE ITS CLOSE

It is tempting to assume that ED refers to the departure of Charles Wadsworth for San Francisco in 1862 and his death in 1882, but, as Thomas Johnson says, 'any speculation about its autobiographical import is vain'.

179. THE RETICENT VOLCANO KEEPS

Cf. letter to Theodore Holland, 1885: 'Vesuvius don't talk—Aetna don't. One of them said a syllable, a thousand years ago, and Pompeii heard it and hid for ever.'

INDEX OF POEMS

112